The Mystics Who Came to Dinner

The Mystics Who Came to Dinner

Carmel Bendon

ORBIS BOOKS

Maryknoll, New York 10545

Manufactured in the United States of America

Library of Congress Cataloging-in-Publication Data

Names: Davis, Carmel Bendon, author.
Title: The mystics who came to dinner / Carmel Bendon.
Description: Maryknoll, New York : Orbis Books, [2022] | Includes
  bibliographical references. | Summary: "Brings together St. Francis of
  Assisi, St. Hildegard of Bingen, Julian of Norwich, Richard Rolle,
  the author of *The Cloud of Unknowing*, and Margery Kempe for dinner
  and lively conversation in a modern home setting" — Provided by publisher.
Identifiers: LCCN 2021035129 (print) | LCCN 2021035130 (ebook) | ISBN
  9781626984530 (print) | ISBN 9781608339167 (ebook)
Subjects: LCSH: Mystics—Biography. | Church history—Middle Ages,
  600-1500—Biography.
Classification: LCC BV5095.A1 D38 2022 (print) | LCC BV5095.A1 (ebook) |
  DDC 248.2/2—dc23
LC record available at https://lccn.loc.gov/2021035129
LC ebook record available at https://lccn.loc.gov/2021035130

To my husband, Adrian
—my favorite dinner companion

Contents

Acknowledgments

Nearly two decades ago, the late Dr. Sophie McGrath, RSM, co-founder of the Golding Centre at Australian Catholic University (Sydney), invited me to present a paper at the then-annual Women's History Conference. I obliged, and we became friends who met regularly to discuss our "big ideas." It was Sophie who first encouraged me to write about the mystics for a contemporary audience. Other projects pushed the mystics to the back of the line and it was not until Sophie's death in June 2020 that I became determined to "get serious" about finding a way to write the book we had so often discussed. I know that she would be pleased that I have finally completed the task, and I send prayers and thanks to her for all her support and encouragement for this, and other pursuits, over the years.

Thank you to Adrian, Laura, Erin, Bridget, Ben, and Delfina—shining souls, who also happen to be my family—for their love and support over many years and for their unfailing confidence in me and in this book. Special thanks to my husband, Adrian, whose insightful feedback on earlier drafts of the manuscript was invaluable.

Thank you to Dianne Masri, Michele Seminara, Amanda Hickey, and Adriana Cortazzo—creative colleagues, willing sounding boards, and divine friends—for keeping me focused, keeping me positive, and always asking the right questions.

Thank you to Orbis Books, especially editor-in-chief Robert Ellsberg, for his enthusiastic acceptance of this book; and to Paul McMahon for his thoughtful editing; and to the Orbis Books staff in general for their diligent work in the publication of this book.

Lastly, but by no means least, thank you to Hildegard, Francis, Richard, Cloud, Julian and Margery, whose brilliant writings and exceptional lives have comforted, guided, and inspired me over many years, and who, eventually, wore me down and persuaded me to invite them home to dinner and to commit their conversations to print for others to enjoy.

Introduction

In 1141, the Rhineland abbess Hildegard of Bingen was overcome by a barrage of bright lights that flickered wildly in front of her eyes, gradually spreading a terrible pain throughout her head before coalescing into a dance of visions that shone with vibrant colors and multi-dimensional shapes.

Two and a half centuries later, in the east of England, the thirty-year-old Julian of Norwich was also transfixed by bright lights in the form of a beam of radiance that focused on the suddenly vivified figure of a dying Jesus Christ on the cross.

Not long afterwards, and not far from Norwich in the English market town of Bishop's Lynn, Margery Kempe, mother of a newborn baby, experienced the extreme upheaval of being unable to carry on with her home life because she was beset by terrifying demonic visions that only ceased when Jesus appeared to her. Not many years before Margery's upheaval, in the English midlands, the unknown man who would write *The Cloud of Unknowing* was settling into his contemplative life that he lived "between two clouds," while around the same time in England's Yorkshire area, the young Richard Rolle had stripped off his own clothes, donned his sister's tunic and his father's rain hood, and fled to the woods to live as a solitary hermit. Much earlier, in twelfth century Umbria (in present-day Italy) the young Francis of Assisi had also stripped off his clothes in the most public of places—Assisi's town square—before dressing in rags and leaving everything to live in poverty.

Modern-day interpretations of the strange behavior, and of the lights and pain and visions, reported by this group of men and women centuries ago, tend to center on the likely pathology of such physical and perceptual disturbances. "Migraine," declare neurologists who have considered Hildegard's symptoms. "Ergot poisoning," proffer physicians who have studied Julian's descriptions of her pain. "Post-partum depression," psychiatrists say of Margery Kempe's break with reality, while Saint Francis, Richard Rolle, and the author of *The Cloud of Unknowing* (referred to henceforth also as the *Cloud* author) are ripe for labeling with any number of neurotic or psychotic diagnoses. And the neurologists, physicians, and psychiatrists might well be correct, if these symptoms and signs were the end of the stories. However, these signs, in fact, were only the beginning, only the precipitators, of something that had very little to do with disease processes and everything to do with the elaboration of a richly detailed and complete world of visionary and mystical experiences that, once committed to writing by the men and women who received them, would survive to the present day and propel their recipients into the bright lights of twenty-first century recognition.

Saints Francis of Assisi and Hildegard of Bingen, along with Julian of Norwich, Richard Rolle, Margery Kempe, and the *Cloud* author, as well as many other men and women like them, are often categorized today under the collective label of "medieval mystics." The term "medieval" is relatively straightforward and refers to that long sweep of human history between the early fifth century AD (when the Western Roman Empire finally fell to the Visigoths) and the dawning of the Renaissance in the fifteenth century. However, in situating these mystics throughout that long-ago period, it is perhaps understandable that we might regard them as unusual individuals who have little or no relevance to our current lives and experiences. But it is only the term "medieval" that fixes them in time. The term, "mystics," is more transferable in that it is not exclusive to the medieval period. Across the centuries, mystics have been, and are still today, a feature of the world's major religions.

Broadly, a "mystic" is defined as one who experiences a personal and unmediated apprehension of the Divine. But what does this mean? The word "mysticism" comes from the Indo-European root *mu*, which is a transcription (and imitation) of the inarticulate sounds that are pre-language. We sometimes speak of babies "mewing" (and we say that cows "moo"). From that root word, too, we derive words like "mute" and "mystery," and what we are really referring to is something that is beyond language, beyond ready explanation. Thus, "mysticism" means an experience, any experience, any "knowing" that is before, after, above, below, or beyond language; it is the experience of the "inexpressible," but it is no less real and valid than the countless things to which language gives voice.

We have all had experiences that are difficult, even impossible, to put into words, occurrences that seem to come "out of the blue," disrupting—or sometimes enhancing—our lives and making us question not only long-held beliefs but also the very nature of reality. For all of us, there are experiences that shake us, frighten us out of our customary patterns of thought and action. Such an experience may be the onset of a serious illness or the loss of a loved one. Sometimes it may be something much more subtle but unsettling, nevertheless. For example, have you ever looked at something very familiar but suddenly seen it in a new way? Or maybe you have caught a movement out of the corner of your eye that seems real but is so fleeting that you are not quite sure you have really seen anything. Perhaps you have had the coincidence of bumping into a friend you haven't seen for years but were just thinking about minutes before, or maybe you hear your long-departed mother's favorite song from decades ago playing on the radio when you start the car on the morning of her birthday. Some people speak of an uneasy feeling in the pit of their stomach a few hours before getting the news that a loved one has passed away, or a dream so vivid that they can't stop thinking about it the next day.

It is that intrusion of "otherness" into our ordinary everyday life that pulls us up, makes us stop in our tracks and wonder, even if only for a moment, before we resume the headlong rush toward the next thing we need to do. But for that moment, we are seeing things differently; in that moment we are experiencing the unexplainable, the inexpressible, and the mysterious. We are experiencing something mystical. In this sense, we are all mystics, but those who are specifically called "mystics" are those who, having had an experience where eternity seems to break through into the everyday, set about communicating—usually in writing—that experience for the benefit of others.

That benefit is almost as difficult to express as the description of the mystical experience itself, because mystics, in their divine apprehensions, experience nothing less than the essence of being, and that essence is God. Theirs are the visions, auditions, and perceptions of the Divine reality. What they gain is the certainty that a bigger, more expansive life of the spirit exists beyond the boundaries of our five senses. It is the certainty of an immanent and transcendent God—always present in and to us. And with this comes the unerring conviction that such insights are not given for the individual mystic's benefit alone but for the benefit of all. Within each mystic's quiet, personal experience is the accompanying imperative to share it with others, with all who are open and willing to receive the insights.

The mystics' challenge, then, is finding the best way to effect that sharing, that communication, because, as we have discussed, what they have experienced is essentially beyond language, beyond accurate description. For all mystics, the attempt to describe what they have experienced is at best an approximation, a shadowy sketching of an ineffable reality. Francis of Assisi, Hildegard of Bingen, Julian of Norwich, the *Cloud* author, Margery Kempe, and Richard Rolle faced this dilemma in their own day; the passing of many centuries has only magnified the difficulty. Nevertheless, if an insight is divinely given, divinely true, then it is true not only in the time in which it is received but for all times. Truth is not defined by a particular decade, or century, nor confined to a particular place. It follows, then, that when the medieval mystics offer the "fruit" of their experience, it is "fruit freely given" as a gift for our modern sustenance, too. What they teach stretches across the centuries to be as relevant today as it was in the twelfth, thirteenth, and fourteenth centuries.

However, for us today, engaging with something that was first experienced and shared hundreds of years ago comes with its own particular problems, one of the most fundamental being the strangeness of the medieval period itself to our contemporary understanding. Yes, it was a time of knights and ladies, castles, monks and monasteries—these are the popular (and appealing) images of the era. But the reality of life then was actually much harsher, with poor hygiene, crowded living conditions, a short life expectancy, a meager diet, diseases, pestilence, plagues, high mortality from illness in the general populace and from childbirth for women, illiteracy in all but the highest social and clerical classes, and the suppression of women in all sectors of society. And, of course, there were the extreme expressions of religious piety, which included the religious vocation of anchorites and anchoresses—those hundreds of men and women who willingly underwent a Mass for the Dead before being locked away for life in a tiny cell on the side of a church, or in openings in town walls, or in other cramped spaces; and also the hermits and hermitesses, who settled on a solitary life in caves or other isolated places. Then there were the heretics, who were brought under control by inquisitors and the application of bizarre tortures and state-administered death penalties; and adherence to beliefs and practices that included stringent mortification and penances, long and dangerous pilgrimages, adoration of relics, and more. We can only begin to imagine what medieval life was really like—the joys, sorrows, and hardships that accompanied people from cradle to grave.

Strange, too, to our modern sensibilities, and our strong (and appropriate) adherence to science and its methods and objectivity, is the notion of a mystical experience which, by definition, is personal, experiential, and subjective. We are rightly cautious about accepting claims of unusual occurrences that are not amenable to rational proof. At the same time, however, we acknowledge that there are other ways of "knowing," "being," and "experiencing" that are not squarely based on reason. Our emotions, for example, often prompt us to act irrationally. We are moved to love, to hate, to fear, to dream, and while science might seek to give explanations of such things, the range and depth of human actions and reactions cannot be verified solely by recourse to empirical methods. The beauty of the natural world, the expanse of the cosmos, the vibrancy of human creativity also point to something that is far beyond the rational. Art, music, and poetry are among those things that speak to us in symbols that evoke our deepest emotions. We know these things are real—sometimes more real than the daily routine of eat-sleep-work that we move through almost mechanically—and it is nature, the arts, the emotions that can make us feel most alive, most in tune with ourselves and engaged with others. Again, such feeling and engagement is often not amenable to rational explanation nor to expression in straightforward language.

Similarly, the mystical experience takes the individual by surprise, snapping attachment to routine. It is not surprising, then, that mystics use symbolic language frequently in their texts to convey their ideas and insights. "Music of the spheres," the "fire of love," the "cloud of unknowing," "*viriditas*," "heavenly merriment," "God, our mother," "brother sun, sister moon" are a few of the many phrases that mystics have used to point to that which is beyond language, and to express the inexpressible.

In turn, something very interesting often happens when we hear, read, or pray with these and other symbolic phrases: our usual attachments to everyday language are disrupted and, not unlike the mystics themselves, we are drawn away from the material to the spiritual, from the literal to the metaphorical, from the ordinary to the extraordinary "otherness" of life. We start to see things differently, just as the mystics did.

As it happens, this is a vital step in the mystics' communication of their received truth because, as we know, all communication is a two-way process. The dissemination of mystical insights is pointless, meaningless, unless those insights find an audience, stir a spark of interest or empathy in others. That is, for the communication of their experiences to be effective, the mystics require something from us. They need us to meet them halfway; to take the gift they offer and to unpack it with care. Their messages are not like slick advertisements that promise quick solutions. Really, they are threads of ideas, tails of dreams, wisps of truth caught in another dimension, packages of gossamer that the mystics have tried to transfer into a language that does not have words for the things they have seen and experienced. But, if we approach the mystics with an open heart and mind, with curiosity and respect, we might find that, like immersing ourselves in beautiful art or in music or in nature, we come to understand more deeply something of the human spirit—that part of us that is crafted in the divine image. We need to approach with humility, as we would when meeting someone for the first time, as we might chat to guests in our home, and with enough respect to put aside prejudgment, especially around the limitations and restrictions that the medieval way of living and thinking imposed upon the people of that time.

And that's why I've invited the mystics to dinner. In our imaginations, at some stage, we have probably all answered—or at least thought about—the hypothetical question of which celebrities or historical persons we would like to have dinner with, without any limitations with regard to time or place. In this game of the imagination, royalty, inventors, actors, writers, artists, explorers are always popular dinner guest choices. I decided that sharing a meal with a group of mystics, without the constraints of the medieval times in which they first felt the divine call, would allow their personalities to shine beyond the flat pages of their texts, enable discussion around the essentials of their spirituality, and let us have a fireside seat as they share the relevance of their mystical insights with us, God's people of the twenty-first century. Of course, dinner guests can be unpredictable, and the mystics might choose to discuss something of the challenges of living in the Middle Ages but, for the most part, I am guessing that the focus of their sharing will be around the insights and lessons they received in their mystical experiences, and the ways in which those insights and lessons are transferable and relevant to living authentic, full lives, today. I'm presuming that the guests will not cover every aspect of their mystical and visionary lives because, after all, it's a dinner party conversation, not a lecture. I'm confident, though, that the extraordinary gift of their insights and lessons will be repackaged in modern wrapping so that while the gift—the truth of their experiences—is the same across time, the updated wrapping will make it easier to open and to appreciate that gift.

I'm certain, too, that they will be totally honest and that, in their open-hearted honesty, they will invite us to share in the human experience of mystery across the centuries and, hopefully, come to a clearer understanding of our own inner lives and to an awareness of the mystic within each of us.

The Dinner Guests

I invited Francis of Assisi, Hildegard of Bingen, Julian of Norwich, Richard Rolle, *The Cloud of Unknowing* author, and Margery Kempe as my guests because, over many years, their writings have fascinated, challenged, comforted, and inspired me. I have been privileged to share their writings and spirituality with academic and general audiences, always to warm appreciation for the insights and blessings that these great medieval mystics bring. Over the years, too, I've come to know these three women and three men not only as extraordinary mystics but also as unique individuals, each with their own lifestyle, spiritual practice, and personality. These intriguing men and women will, no doubt, tell us more about their lives and vocations as the evening progresses but, as would be the case with any guest coming into our homes, we first like to know a little about them. Here, then, are a few general biographical details about our dinner companions.

SAINT FRANCIS OF ASSISI

Francis was born in 1181 to Pietro di Bernadone and his wife, Pica, in Umbria (present-day Italy). Pietro, a cloth merchant, is said to have named his son "Francesco" (Francis) in honor of his business dealings in France. As a young man, Francis enjoyed the wild social life that his family's wealth allowed, but he also had an adventurous streak and, in 1201, went off to fight in a civil war. This proved a bad decision when Francis was captured by the enemy and imprisoned for a year, being released only when his wealthy father paid his ransom. Not deterred by the experience of captivity, Francis set off in 1204 to enlist for the Fourth Crusade. However, en route he experienced strange dreams and visions and, unable to continue with his journey, returned to Assisi to work in his father's cloth trade.

Francis could not settle in this work and began wandering alone in the hills above Assisi where, one day in 1205, he found himself gazing at a crucifix in the old church of San Damiano. As he gazed, the figure of Christ spoke to him, instructing him to repair the church. Francis took the directive literally and set about repairing, stone by stone, the crumbling little church, paying for the repairs by selling his horse and some of his father's most expensive cloth. His father, angered by Francis's actions, took him before the town's council. In response to charges leveled against him, Francis stripped himself bare, giving back the clothes provided to him by his father, and declaring that henceforth his life would be dedicated to God. From then on, Francis dressed in rags and went about begging for his food, preaching poverty and the love of God.

Soon, others joined him. From late 1209 to early 1210, Francis and eleven brothers traveled to Rome to seek papal permission to establish a new religious order. At first, the pope refused, but then he had a dream in which he saw Francis propping up a crumbling church—and not just a single edifice, but the whole institution. So, in April 1210, Pope Innocent III gave verbal approval for the establishment of the Order of Friars Minor (later, the "Franciscans"). As more men joined Francis and the brothers, they set about preaching far and wide, even going into Egypt and the Holy Land in 1219. It is said that Francis preached to anyone and anything, including animals. When Francis's health and eyesight began to decline, he retreated from his extensive preaching, spending more time in solitary contemplation.

Francis died on Saturday, October 3, 1226, at age forty-five, and two years later, in 1228, he was canonized by Pope Gregory IX. In 1939, Francis was proclaimed a patron saint of Italy and, in 1980, he was declared the patron saint of ecology. He is also the patron saint of animals. His feast day is October 4. In 2013, Jorge Bergoglio took the name "Francis" on his election to the papacy.

SAINT HILDEGARD OF BINGEN

Hildegard was born in 1098 in Bermerscheim, not far from modern-day Mainz, in the German Rhineland, and was one of several children of a noble, well-to-do family. According to one of her hagiographers, Godfrey of Disibodenberg, Hildegard displayed such remarkable holiness from a very young age that her parents dedicated her to a religious life when she was only seven years old. This dedication involved having Hildegard enclosed with the anchoress,[1] Jutta, in a cell attached to the local Benedictine monastery. From Jutta, Hildegard, in the company of other young girls also in Jutta's care, received a basic education and instruction in the religious life. At some point, Jutta and her group moved from the anchorhold (a dwelling of an anchorite or anchoress) to a convent under the auspices of the local Benedictine monks in Disibodenberg. When she was about fifteen years old, Hildegard took the veil and became a Benedictine nun and, when Jutta died in 1136, Hildegard assumed leadership of the convent.

In 1141, visions that Hildegard had experienced for much of her life intensified and were brought to the attention of Pope Eugenius, who instructed that Hildegard should record the visions in detail. Thus began Hildegard's lifelong writing career and the production of the wide range

---

1. A definition of "anchoress" (male equivalent "anchorite") and a description of the anchoress's lifestyle is given by the character, Julian, in the soup chapter.

of amazing works, the most substantial being the *Scivias*, in which Hildegard describes a series of lucid visions with full theological explication. The following list of Hildegard's known works attests to the range of her knowledge, skill, and creativity:

The Visionary Trilogy
Liber scivias domini (Know the Ways of the Lord)
Liber vitae meritorum (Book of Life's Merits)
Liber divinorum operum (Book of the Divine Works)

Natural Science
Liber subtilitatum diversarum naturum creaturam (Book on the Subtleties of Many Kinds of Creatures)
Physica or Liber simplices medicinae (Book of Simple Medicine)
Causae et curae or Liber compositae medicinae (Book of Compound Medicine)

Miscellaneous Works
Expositiones evangeliorum (Discourses on the Gospels)
Litterae ignotae (Cryptic Writings)
Lingua ignota (Cryptic Language)
Explanatio regulae Sancti Benedictini (Explanation of the Rule of St. Benedict)
Explanatio symboli Sancti Athanasii (Explanation of the Symbols of St. Athanasius)
Vita Sancti Ruperti (Life of St. Rupert)
Vita Sancti Disibodi (Life of St. Disibod)

> *Solutiones triginta octo questionum (Solutions to Thirty-Eight Questions)*
> *Epistolae (Letters)*

Play
> *Ordo Virtutum (Play of the Virtues)*

Musical Works
> *Compositions,* collectively called *Symphonia armonie celestium revelationum (Symphony of the Harmony of Celestial Revelations)*

Hildegard died in 1179. Her heart and tongue are preserved in a golden reliquary in the Rüdesheim parish church. Although she has been recognized locally as a saint since the twelfth century, she was officially canonized on May 10, 2012, and on October 7, later that same year, Pope Benedict XVI named Hildegard a Doctor of the Church (one of only four women Doctors of the Church, among thirty-five male Doctors). Her feast day is September 17.

RICHARD ROLLE, HERMIT OF HAMPOLE

Richard Rolle, mystic and prolific writer, was born ca.1300 in Thornton-le-dale in Yorkshire, England. As a young man he studied at the University of Oxford but, before achieving his master's degree, he abandoned his studies and returned to Yorkshire to take up the life of a hermit.

Many of the details of Richard's life are recorded by Richard himself in his semi-autobiographical work *Incendium Amoris.* Originally written in Latin, it was translated after his death and circulated in English as *The Fire of Love*. Although this work is often considered to be lacking in organization and cohesion by modern readers, there is no question that Richard describes his mystical experiences, particularly his apprehensions of *calor*, *canor*, and *dulcor* (warmth, song/melody, and sweetness), with great clarity and enthusiasm. In addition, his dedication to the prayerful and largely solitary life of a hermit is believed to have inspired him to write texts of guidance for women living as nuns or those who were entering into the solitary life of an anchoress. These works were all written in English and include *Ego Dormio*, *The Commandment*, and *The Form of Living*. His other works include extensive commentaries and treatises. Overall, Richard Rolle's influence and popularity as a spiritual writer, not only during the latter part of his own lifetime but also for more than a century following his death, are evidenced by the survival to the present day of over four hundred copies of his works produced throughout England between 1390 and about 1500.

He died in 1349, possibly as a result of the bubonic plague (the "Black Death"), which was raging in England at the time. He was buried at Hampole and a shrine was dedicated to him there. The nuns of Hampole composed a *legenda* in the expectation of his canonization.[2] Reported miracles at his tomb strengthened this expectation, but it was never realized.

---

2. A *legenda* is a book of lessons prepared after a holy person's death in the expectation that this person's holiness in life will be recognized and that canonization will follow. The *legenda* will often form part of the daily prayers of those petitioning for the canonization.

THE CLOUD OF UNKNOWING *AUTHOR*

The anonymous author of the influential work on contemplation *The Cloud of Unknowing* is also the author of several other works on mystical theology, including *The Epistle of Privy Counsel, Dionysius's Mystical Teaching, The Epistle of Discretion in the Stirrings of the Soul,* and *The Treatise of the Discerning of Spirits.* In his writings, the author gives little clue as to his identity beyond indicating that the guidance he offers in *The Cloud of Unknowing* is based on his own experience of the contemplative life. It has been variously speculated, and argued, that the author was a secular priest, a monk, a Carthusian, a hermit, a recluse, a country parson, but none of these can be proven. The only facts about this author are to be adduced from his texts, which he wrote in a particular (English) dialect, suggesting that he was of an East Midlands (England) background. Furthermore, reference in his works to other (known) authors of the time and, in turn, references to *The Cloud of Unknowing* author's texts by later medieval spiritual writers such as Walter Hilton, put the time of composition of his works between 1349 and 1395.

JULIAN OF NORWICH

Biographical details about Julian of Norwich are limited and come mainly from her own writings. An exact birthdate is not known, but in the account of her mystical experiences Julian records that her *Showings* (also known as *Revelations of Divine Love*) began on May 8, 1373, and that, at the time, she was thirty and a half years of age.[3] This gives a birth year of

---

3. Some scholars regard May 13 and not May 8 as the date of the beginning of Julian's revelations. This discrepancy of opinion arises from

late 1342 or early 1343. At some stage of her life, most probably after receiving the revelations, Julian became an anchoress, enclosed in the Church of St. Julian in Carrow, Norwich, in England. It seems likely that Julian took her name from this church (as was common practice among anchoresses of the fourteenth century), which means that we do not even know her real (birth) name. Similarly, her date of death is unknown, but parish records of the time show that she was still alive in 1416 because, in that year, small bequests were made to her in two local wills, with the money going toward her upkeep as the church's anchoress. Julian wrote about the manner of reception and the details of her revelations in two forms: what we now call the *Short Text*, which was written very soon after the receipt of the revelations, and the *Long Text* which, with its expanded details of the original showings and considerable theological reflection on the initial content of the showings, was written up to twenty years after the short version. Julian wrote in Middle English and is credited as being the first (known) female author in English.

Margery Kempe

It is a matter of historical record that Margery was born in 1373 in the Norfolk market town of Bishop's Lynn (now King's Lynn) where her father, John Brunham, was mayor for five separate terms, and that, at the age of twenty,

---

different readings of the date on certain manuscripts due to lack of clarity of the Roman numerals used. Some scholars consider that what looks like an '8' (VIII) could actually be '13' (XIII) with the lower half of the X having been erased or worn away over time. I consider May 8 to be the more likely date.

Margery married John Kempe and, within a year of the marriage, had given birth to their first child. Details after that come from Margery's own account of her life in what is called *The Book of Margery Kempe.* Here she explains that although she and her husband went on to have a further thirteen children, it was the first birth that was especially decisive as, immediately following it, Margery experienced terrifying visions and fiendish torments of such severity that she was unable to look after herself, her child, or her household. Relief from the torment came in the form of a personal visit from Jesus. Extraordinary as this visit seemed to the young Margery, she was an entrepreneurial woman by nature and saw her return to health as a sign that she should turn her hand to commercial ventures such as brewing and milling.

The complete failure of these ventures, coupled with a further spiritual experience in the form of an auditory preview of the bliss of heaven, pushed Margery to dedicate her life to God. Her commitment took an extreme form with incessant praying, daily confession, the wearing of a hair shirt, and rigorous fasting, among other practices. Much of her subsequent life was spent attempting to gain validation of her experiences and official sanction for her adopted lifestyle. One of those from whom she sought validation was Julian of Norwich, and Margery's account of their meeting (c. 1413) provides the only contemporary eyewitness account of Julian giving direct advice to visitors at her anchorhold window.

Margery's travels took her much farther than Norwich, however, and her descriptions of the journeys and pilgrimages all over England, and as far afield as Rome and Jerusalem, mark her as an intrepid woman as well as the author of the first autobiography in English. The date of her death is not known, but Margery was still alive in 1438 when she is recorded as having been admitted to the Guild of the Trinity in Lynn. One further, and final, mention of her—again in relation to the Guild—is made on May 22, 1439.

FACT AND FICTION

The idea of six medieval mystics attending a present-day dinner party is obviously the creation of the author, but it is based firmly on the lives and writings of the six mystics who are the "guests." That is, all the events and conversations during the dinner party are, of course, inventions but, as far as the author's knowledge and skill allows, they are, in general content, authentic representations of many of the recorded events of the guests' lives and of the essential topics at the core of their writings and spiritual experiences, albeit updated, synthesized, and elaborated by the author for the purpose of enhancing engagement with those essential topics in line with twenty-first century experiences and concerns, and in the spirit of a creative work. Broader discussion topics derived from the mystics' central ideas are inventions of the author, and general information and discussion about aspects of medieval life are drawn from the author's knowledge of the period.

While it is a matter of historical record that Julian of Norwich and Margery Kempe met around 1413 when Margery went to Julian's anchorhold to discuss spiritual matters, and while Margery records some details of this meeting in her autobiography,[4] the two women were not known to each other

---

4. Margery records the visit to, and conversation with, Julian in her autobiography. See Margery Kempe, *The Book of Margery Kempe*, ed.

outside this one formal consultation. Nor were any of the other mystics known to each other, though it is possible that Julian of Norwich, Richard Rolle, and the *Cloud* author were familiar with the historical details of Saint Francis of Assisi, who had been canonized in 1228. Furthermore, the Franciscan order was well established in England as well as on the Continent by the fourteenth century. Margery Kempe even lists Assisi as a destination on one of her many pilgrimages. It is possible, too, that the writings of the earlier mystics may have been known to some of the later mystics but nowhere in the mystics' works is this reliably attested. Other than those connections, the guests and the host get to know each other through the course of the evening.

Footnotes have been kept to a minimum to provide, as far as possible, a seamless account of an enjoyable dinner party for readers. However, the direct quotes used in the story are duly acknowledged in footnotes. Also included in footnotes and the Glossary are explanatory comments on unusual or particular aspects of life in the Middle Ages.

Sanford Brown Meech, EETS OS 293 (London: Oxford University Press, 1997), 42.

Arrival

*The guests arrive and
something of their personalities is revealed.*

The heavy rain surprised me. I had imagined that the
evening would be fine and clear, perfect weather for
greeting my guests as they strolled under a beaming moon to
the front porch. It was cool, of course, being late autumn,
but I had accommodated this seasonal fact by turning up the
heating system's temperature a couple of degrees and even
taking time in the afternoon to set a fire in the fireplace in the
living room. It was warm and glowing now, with the wood
that had dried over a long, hot summer, crackling and popping as the vibrant flame devoured it. But that rain! There
would be no strolling to the front door. Instead, there would
be rushing on a puddled path, slippery with soaked fallen
leaves, and wet shoes, damp coats, and dripping umbrellas.

I confess that the downpour added to my already ram-
pant nervousness about the dinner. When I'd originally
thought of the idea of inviting six medieval mystics to enjoy
a modern home-cooked meal and to discuss whatever aspects
of their lives and mystical insights they cared to share with
me, and with each other, my excitement had overshadowed

my reason. It was only when all six so readily accepted the invitation that, day and night, my mind conjured innumerable and torturous scenarios of ways in which it could all go wrong. Topping the "disaster chart" was the possibility that they might just not like each other. And, yes, though they had their mystical experiences in common, their differences in language and age might make conversation impossible. Several hundred years separated them—and even then, they were all from hundreds of years before my time. How would they communicate? What would they say to me? To each other? What would they eat and drink? How adequate was my catering, my cooking?

Sure, as you'd expect, I'd gone to the university library and consulted food records of various medieval monasteries. At home, I'd scoured online blogs about modern-day so-called medieval banquets. I knew that monastic diets were largely vegetarian, but I also discovered that "meat" for the medieval eater referred only to quadrupeds and so, technically, chicken—being two-legged—was probably acceptable. Still, I'd decided to play it very safe and, after much deliberation, had opted to give a modern twist to ingredients that would be familiar to the medieval palate by beginning the meal with a hearty vegetable soup and crusty bread, followed by a main course of baked fish served with a barley, spinach, and mushroom "risotto," along with a leafy greens and fig salad and an apple tart for dessert. Wine and beer—medieval staples—were easy beverage choices, and some pre-dinner snacks of cheese and olives also seemed like good options.

And now, the evening of the dinner is here. The table is set: napkins, flowers, serving spoons, glasses, even candles to remind my guests of their medieval abodes.

The doorbell rings. A shot of panic darts up my spine. I'm frozen to the floor. What am I doing? For a millisecond, I consider ignoring the bell and sprinting out the back door, away from this whole crazy scheme. Good manners rouse me on the bell's second trill and I'm at the door, opening it, my heart pounding.

There, in the flickering yellow of the porch light, and against a background of sheeting rain, stands a tall, heavy-set woman, shrouded—body and face—in a dark brown, woolen cloak.

"Welcome. I'm Annie. Please come in out of the rain, and let me take your cloak," I say, my mouth on auto-pilot. The woman steps across the threshold and, placing a black leather bag on the floor, proceeds to remove her rain-streaked cloak.

"Here, let me help you," I offer.

"No need," the woman replies. "I am able." And, true to her word, she maneuvers the cloak off in one deft tug to reveal a broad face with strong cheek bones, small dark eyes, and wrinkles that indicate an age of about sixty to seventy years. She is wearing a calf-length plaid shift-dress atop a thick cream-colored sweater and, wrapped around her head and tied in a large knot above her right ear, is a brightly patterned scarf from under which wisps of gray hair have escaped. "Thank you, however, for your kind offer of assistance." She smiles, flashing small even teeth at me. I detect an accent in her clipped words but cannot place its provenance. "Hildegard. Hildegard von Bingen," she announces, grabbing my hand in hers and shaking it in a robust and surprisingly strong salute of introduction.

"I'm, I'm, I'm honored . . . to meet you . . . to have you in my home. So honored." My words are sticking to my tongue.

"No. No. It is my honor to be here. Few people of this or any other century have extended me such a generous invitation. I am delighted to be here. We have much to talk about. Now, move away from the door. You will catch your death of cold."

It is a friendly command, but a command nonetheless, and I snap to obedience. "Oh, my apologies. Yes, let's move by the fire." I motion in the direction of the living room with one hand, while hanging her cloak on the coat stand with the other. Hildegard bends down to pick up her carry bag and then strides off ahead of me to take a seat in a comfy, high-backed armchair to the right of the fireplace.

"Can I offer you a drink, Hildegard? I mean, Saint Hildegard, or Abbess Hildegard, or. . . ." I trip over myself in nervous confusion.

"We are friends. Call me Hildegard. No formality. A goblet of red wine, thank you."

I hurry off and return with a glass of my best merlot, and with just enough time to hand it to her before the doorbell sounds again.

Still nervous, I open the door again. A gust of wind rushes in and with it, an unkempt young man in jeans and a torn, gray sweater. His long brown hair is sodden, sticking to his scalp and dripping at his shoulders.

"Oh dear. You're soaked to the skin," I say, as I usher him in, out of the cold.

"Yeah, sorry. I had to run from the train station. But I'm stoked about the invitation." He smiles warmly at me, his handsome face and wide brown eyes alight with what looks like sincere happiness to be in my home. Still smiling, he introduces himself: "Francis . . . of Assisi."

"Oh my goodness. It's wonderful that you could come to dinner. But, please, let me get you some dry clothes. And a towel for your hair. Then you can warm up by the fire."

"Yeah, I'd appreciate the towel but don't worry about the clothes. If it's all right with you, I'm going to take off my wet sneakers, and leave them at the door, so I don't wreck your carpet. And then I'll just sit by the fire and dry off there."

I nod and hurry to get a towel. By the time I return, Francis has disappeared. And then, hearing laughter coming from the living room, I sprint in that direction to find him sitting cross-legged on the floor close to the fire and chatting animatedly with Hildegard.

"Do you two know each other?" I ask, taking a seat opposite them.

"Interesting question," says Hildegard, tilting her head to one side. "And interesting coincidence: Francis was born in 1181, just two years after I left mortal life in 1179. So let us just say we were not acquainted during our earthly lives, but we certainly know each other's souls."

My curiosity is put on hold by the chiming of the doorbell again. I excuse myself, but Francis and Hildegard have already returned to their conversation. This time, there are two people huddled under one umbrella on my porch. Two women. One is of medium height, slender, finely boned; the other is quite short and very stout.

"Come in out of this terrible weather," I urge, opening the door wide until they're safely across the threshold and then shutting the door firmly behind them, closing off a biting wind that has found its way into my front garden, pushing more rain with it.

"Thank you, thank you," shouts the stout woman, removing her overcoat and shaking the water from it. "Oops, apologies for dampening your floor here. Mind if I remove my shoes?" she asks and, without waiting for my agreement, she leans one hand on the wall to steady herself as she works one ankle boot off with the other foot and then repeats the process with the second shoe. Shoes to the side, she wriggles two red-stockinged feet but does not pause for breath before her booming voice continues, "Dreadful evening to be out. Oh, not to be disrespectful to you, our kind hostess, I presume, but it took some persuading by my friend here to coax me away from my hearth and into that Uber tonight, I can tell you. In any case, here we are. And it's a lovely warm house, isn't it. And a meal with friends is always a blessing. So, let's forget all about the weather and begin our evening. Here you are, my dear. Just a little something from my brewery for you." She thrusts a small carry bag into my hands and, feeling its weight and hearing bottles clinking, I guess that it's beer.

"Thank you, Margery? Margery Kempe?" I ask, already knowing the answer.

"Yes, dear. Who else would I be? Oh, oh surely not?" she laughs. "Did you think I was Julian?" She pivots to the slender woman who, during Margery's effusive greeting, has stood motionless and quietly a little behind her friend. She is still in her coat and is holding a little posy of violets in one hand, a small leather-bound book in the other.

I step forward to acknowledge her. "Welcome Julian of Norwich," I say. "I have wanted to meet you for such a long time."

Julian smiles and offers the flowers and the book to me, saying, "These are for you, Annie. The violets are from my little anchorhold garden; and I hope you will accept this book of my revelations. I've been copying it for you ever since I received your invitation."

I am so overcome by these rare gifts that it's an effort to remember my role as host but, somehow, I manage to place the book and posy and bag of beer onto the hall stand so that I can help Julian out of her coat. Once it is hung next to Margery's overcoat, I have a moment to step back and take in the two women's appearances. Julian's hair is fair and cropped closely around an oval face of skin so pale that it is almost translucent. The bright blue intelligence of her eyes is unmissable, even though her downcast look suggests a shyness. Her long-sleeved black dress is well cut and of very fine wool, its simplicity highlighting her only piece of jewelry: a small gold crucifix on a slim gold chain around her neck. Margery is Julian's exact complement with her green eyes in a round, ruddy face surrounded by a riot of auburn curls, and an unstructured dress of bold geometric shapes in vivid blues, oranges, and yellows struggling for recognition under the weight of layers of heavy black and red beads around her neck and a forearm of chunky bangles.

"Margery and Julian, I can't believe you're both here. Please, come and meet the others," I say as I retrieve their gifts and turn to lead the way. We only make it to the entrance to the living room when the doorbell chimes once more.

"Go, go," instructs Margery. "No fuss. We can introduce ourselves, can't we, Julian? We've been around long enough to know the ropes."

I do not doubt Margery for a second and, taking her at her word, head for the front door to find a small, neatly built man making his way inside.

"I rang the bell. Wasn't sure if you heard. And then, when I tried knocking, the door opened by itself. I think the latch may be a little loose. Be sure to close it firmly later, won't you? So, here I am. Richard Rolle of Hampole, at your service, Madame. I would take your hand but I see that your arms are full," he declares, noticing the gifts from my earlier guests that I am still carrying. "If I may remove my wet top-coat, I shall assist you."

"Mr. Rolle. Delighted to meet you. I'm Annie. And, yes, of course, please, hang your coat there with the others."

"'Richard' is the preferred mode of address for me this evening, dear Annie," he insists as he turns back to me. He is very smartly dressed in a black lounge suit, peak-collared white shirt and a red bow tie. His black patent leather shoes seem to be perfectly dry, their shine unaffected by the rain. They are almost as shiny as his slick black hair and small black eyes. And when he extends his hands to take the bag of beer from me, I notice that his fingernails are well-manicured and the skin of his hands is as unblemished as his face.

"Lead on at your leisure," he instructs, and I obey.

"If you don't mind, Richard, could we go via the kitchen before I introduce you to the others? I'd first like to put the beer in the fridge and these lovely violets in a vase. It won't take long."

"Of course," he agrees and follows me down the side hallway directly to the kitchen where I put Julian's book on the dresser and grab a vase for the flowers while Richard unloads six bottles of beer onto the counter.

I transfer two of the beers onto a large tray that I had set earlier with glasses, a pitcher of iced water, and a carafe each of red and of white wine, conscious that I need to hurry because only Hildegard, so far, has been given a drink.

"Annie, that tray is too heavy and unwieldy for you. Please, allow me," Richard says, stepping up and assuming control of the tray.

I nod a thank you and take up a plate of cheeses and crackers and olives. Richard and the tray follow me out of the kitchen, through the dining room and into the living room where we place the refreshments on the coffee table in the middle of the guests who are so engrossed in their conversation that they don't appear to realize that Richard and I (and the drinks) have arrived.

"Ahmm," I murmur. "Ahmm," again, a little louder. "Excuse me, sorry to interrupt. I see that you have well and truly introduced yourselves. But, if you will allow me a moment, I'd like to welcome you all to my humble home; to express my gratitude that you are here; and to introduce you all more formally to each other, in case one or two of you are somehow unaware of another's particular place in the rare sphere of mystical endeavor and achievement."

All my guests politely turn their faces in my direction, anticipating my promised introductions. I feel my heart pounding but take a deep breath and announce, "Here, I'd like to introduce our latest arrival, Master Richard Rolle of Hampole. Now, in turn, allow me to present Saint Hildegard of Bingen, Sybil of the Rhine, mystic, visionary, abbess, polymath, musician, natural scientist, and playwright, among other accomplishments. And here is Julian of Norwich, mystic, anchoress, and author of *Showings*, also called *Revelations of Divine Love*. And, from the same era and region of England, this is Margery Kempe, pilgrim, commercial entrepreneur, and author of the first autobiography in English. And this young man by the fire is the great saint, mystic, and founder of the Franciscan order, Saint Francis of Assisi. Now, if I could invite you to help yourself to a drink of your choice from the tray, I'd like to then propose a toast to the success of our evening."

I am gratified to see the guests milling around the coffee table and filling their glasses, chatting as they go. I notice Margery opts for the beer, as does Richard. Julian pours a very small amount of white wine into her glass and tops it up with water. Francis, too, takes the water and wine combination. Hildegard does not hold back in topping up her red wine. It's only when I decide to pour myself a glass of wine that I become aware of someone else in the room, someone I did not welcome at the door nor include in my introductions. The problem with the latch must have enabled him to let himself in while I was in the kitchen after Richard's arrival. I am mortified that this guest has been overlooked. I know exactly who he is. I stop pouring my drink and look up at him as he stands quietly by the bookcase, to the left of the fireplace. He is a man of average size, perhaps mid-fifties, balding, bespectacled, and dressed in corduroy trousers and a navy blue cardigan over a light blue shirt. Without leaving my spot near the table I smile apologetically at him and, to my relief, he smiles back. I motion toward the drinks, pointing first to the water, to which he shakes his head, then to the red wine at which he gives me a "thumbs-up" gesture. I breathe a sigh of gratitude for his kindness over my neglect of him and, pouring a generous glass of wine, I make my way to the bookcase and hand him the drink.

"I cannot tell you how sorry I am to have not noticed you there. Please forgive me and allow me to introduce you to everyone now."

"No apology necessary," he says. "It's really my fault, if any fault is to be attributed. I keep myself to myself, you see. And, though I'm truly glad to be here tonight, I was relieved that the front door was slightly ajar when I arrived so that I could make my way in without fanfare. And, just for your peace of mind, I tightened the latch for you too, so no other surprise guests will appear."

"But, of course, you're not a surprise guest. You were expected. That's why I'm apologizing. I should have acknowledged you earlier."

"Please, no more. I accept your apology and thank you most sincerely for inviting me."

I nod, and we clink glasses. In my effort to make amends, I try to capture the guests' attention by repeating my little "Ahmm" sound and am rewarded by their immediate attention.

"Dear guests, before we raise a glass in the expectation of a wonderful dinner gathering, I must introduce you to one more very important member of our party. This is ... this man here ... he is ... um ... he is the author of some of the best known works of medieval mystical theology, including the revered *The Cloud of Unknowing*." I stop as five inquisitive and amused faces stare at me. Actually, six amused faces, as the man standing next to me is also smiling broadly at my discomfort. Still, he makes no move to help and there is no alternative but for me to ask: "What *is* your name? Your texts are anonymously authored. Today, we just call you 'The Cloud Author.' You see my dilemma. I mean, we can't just call you Mr. Cloud."

"Quite right," he agrees, and stepping in front of me and, addressing the others, he says in a quiet but clear voice, "Let's not get stuck on labels and formality. We are all friends. Please drop the 'Mr.' and just call me 'Cloud.'"

The others laugh and gabble in agreement. Richard approaches to shake Cloud's hand, and then Margery, with a wave of her hand, invites him to sit near her on the sofa. And before I have time for any more discomfort, the party resumes, the conversation intensifies, and laughter is filling the room. I look on in grateful amazement until Francis taps his glass and insists that I join the conversation circle by taking the remaining seat on the sofa and share with my guests my reasons for convening this dinner.

"Well," I begin, the shaking glass in my hand betraying my nervousness, "I have read and admired all your writings, your insights, your devotion. Selfishly, I suppose, I just wanted to meet you all, to hear more about your thoughts and experiences, your spirituality, and your love of God and of others. I believe that your mystical insights, your wisdom, are sorely needed today, and I thought that I should try to have you share with the modern world something of the divine essence that each of you has received. I wondered, given the opportunity, what you would say to us, what you would recommend as a way to find some meaning and purpose now. So, I just sent the invitations out into the 'wild, blue yonder' as they say and, to my joy and utter surprise, you all agreed to attend. And here you are." I finish my little speech, take a gulp of wine, and look around the circle at the fantastic guests gathered in my home.

Hildegard's voice breaks the silence. "I know that I speak for each of your guests, Annie, in saying that we're excited to be here, and that we will do our best to share our God-given insights as thoroughly and clearly as the opportunity allows. As I'm sure you know, the mystical enterprise involves imparting to others all that has been opened to us. We're the messengers, after all, not the message."

There are murmurs of assent all around.

"Thank you," I respond. "Of course, I want you to enjoy yourselves here, too. And part of that enjoyment, I hope, will be the dinner I've prepared for you. I just have a few finishing touches to put to it so, if I can leave you to your drinks and each other for a bit, I'll be ready to call you to the dining room very soon. By the way, down the hallway, second door on the right, is the bathroom and, please, feel free to make your way there if you care to wash before dinner."

More murmurs of assent, and the comments, "Don't go to any trouble with the meal" and "Be sure to enjoy the evening yourself" ring out. As I begin to rise to my feet, Cloud, in his quietly commanding voice, says, "Is there anything you want to ask us before dinner? Any practical questions, for example?"

At that moment, it seems as if Cloud has read my thoughts and given me permission to pose one particular question that has been bothering me about this evening.

"Well, yes, there is," I reply and sit back down on the sofa. "One very big question has been puzzling me—and I hope you will excuse the long prologue to this question. You all lived such a long time ago. Hildegard, not to be disrespectful about your age, but I know you were born in 1098, over nine hundred years ago. And Francis, you're not far behind Hildegard with a birthdate of 1181. As for you, Richard, I think you were born in 1300. Cloud, you're hard to pin down on this, being anonymous, but evidence in your texts puts your birth only a few decades at most after Richard's. Julian, you've said yourself in your texts that you were thirty and a half years old in 1373 so that puts your birth at 1342 or 1343. While Margery, as the daughter of a mayor of Bishop's Lynn, your birthdate of 1373 is a matter of public record. In addition, Francis, your place of birth was Assisi in the Umbria region of modern-day Italy; Hildegard, yours was the Rhineland of today's Germany; Richard, the north of England; Cloud, the English Midlands; and Julian, while we don't know where you were born, we do know that you lived much of your life in Norwich in East Anglia, not so far from Margery's hometown. So, with the exception of Julian and Margery who have a timeframe and dialect in common—but also bearing in mind that the dialect is very different from today's English—you all speak different languages, you've all lived in remote times that bear little resemblance to today and yet, here you are, communicating with me and each other in perfect, contemporary English, dressed in the current fashion, arriving here by train, Uber, or who knows what. Yes, this is a long prologue to my question: How is this possible?"

"All things are possible with God," Hildegard reminds us, assuming the role of speaking on behalf of all the guests. "As you've said in your reasons for inviting us, our works are currently available. Modern audiences read us, engage with us, so that our work is still alive. That keeps us fresh, present. One's age is just a number; age differences are definitely not something we dwell on, so let's dismiss that one. As for the language variations, let's just say that we're adaptable. We're not the sort of people who arrive at someone's home unprepared. We know modern English is really the *lingua franca* of today. We can read the signs, as they say; we can go with the times. We're familiar with some of the modern translations of our works and find them generally acceptable. We received these divine insights for everyone's benefit, you know. And not just 'everyone' in the Middle Ages but everyone...in every time. Relevance is vital."

"Here's to relevance," says Richard, raising his glass. The others are quick to respond and after quite a raucous round of "Hear, hear," my guests are back to animated chatting among themselves. One of them even breaks into a song that, though I am unfamiliar with it, ignites much laughter, and soon more join in the chorus. I'm pleased that my move from the sofa to the kitchen puts no stop on their enjoyment and, as I transfer the warm bread from the oven to a serving basket and begin ladling the hot vegetable soup from the saucepan into the terrine, my smile reflects my inner satisfaction at seeing everyone getting along so well and at the joyful mood that they've all brought to the party. While I'm carrying the bread and soup to the table, something the Cloud author wrote about the disposition of those who devote their lives to the quiet contemplation of God comes into my mind: "Anyone who has...come to the work of contemplation will find their appearance suddenly and graciously changed, so that everyone who sees them will be glad and joyful to have them in their company."[1]

I think, too, of Margery's words after she was quite swept up in ecstasy at hearing the sounds of heaven, telling her husband, "It is full merry in heaven."[2]

It is "full merry" in my home tonight, too, and I'm reluctant to move the party from the comfort of their fireside

---

1. Anonymous. *The Cloud of Unknowing and The Book of Privy Counselling*, ed. Phyllis Hodgson, EETS. o.s. 218 (London: Oxford University Press, 1944), 100. (Trans. of this sentence by Carmel Bendon).

2. Margery Kempe, *The Book of Margery Kempe*, ed., Sanford Brown Meech, EETS o.s. 293 (London: Oxford University Press, 1997), 11.

chairs to the dining room, lest I spoil the mood. Nevertheless, the soup awaits and so, standing at the door of the living room and interrupting with yet another "Ahmm," I invite everyone to make their way to the table. I need not have worried because, as one, it seems, they spring to their feet and proceed in the direction that my extended arm indicates, without breaking their conversations.

Soup

The guests' early life and entry into the mystical life are discussed.

Following my guests from the living room, I call after them to sit in any place they choose. And though they are only steps in front of me, by the time I enter the dining room, they are all comfortably seated around the table, in the arrangement that I had envisaged would be the most appropriate.

"Welcome, again, to my home," I say, as I take my place that my guests have left vacant for me, with Cloud to my right and Francis to my left. "I thought one, or two, of you might say a prayer of blessing for our meal and our gathering here tonight." I glance across at Hildegard, sitting to Cloud's right, thinking that she would be the most likely guest to have something at the ready for this occasion but it is Julian, sitting on Francis's left, who, quietly and deliberately, with head bowed and hands joined, lifts her voice in prayer, saying, "'There was a treasure on earth which the Lord loved . . . a food which was delicious and pleasing to him . . . obtained by the hard labor of a gardener, digging and ditching and sweating.'[1] Thank you, Lord, for the food we are about to eat, for the earth that has nurtured it, for the gardener who labored to harvest it, for our hostess who has worked lovingly to prepare it for us."

A chorus of "Amen" ensues, and then Richard fills the glasses with the wine I had put on the table earlier.

"A toast to our host," Richard announces, and glasses are raised and clinked.

"Thank you. And here's to my extraordinary guests," I respond and begin ladling soup into bowls.

"Pass each bowl to me, and I'll pass them on around the table," says Francis.

"Thanks so much, Francis," I say, turning toward him with the first of the filled bowls. It's then that I notice my dog has decided to join us and has taken up a low-lying position under Francis's chair. The passing of food in his general direction has drawn him out of hiding, and the thumping of his tail on the timber floor in anticipation of any food scraps is a dead giveaway to his uninvited presence. I fix my stare on him and scold, "You know you are not allowed in the dining room. Back to your bed in the kitchen immediately."

"Please don't send him away on our account," says Cloud. "I think we're all fond of dogs here."

"I'd definitely like him to stay," agrees Hildegard. "There's something quite comforting about having a dog around."

---

1. Julian of Norwich. *Showings*, ed. Edmund Colledge and James Walsh, Classics of Western Spirituality Series. (New York: Paulist Press, 1978), 273. Please note that only the first half of this prayer is from Julian. The second half is the author's creative addition to Julian's words.

"I think you could guess my view on the subject," laughs Francis. "What's his name?"

"Pat. Pat the dog," I sigh, realizing the dog has won, easily. Pat knows it, too, and settles back under Francis's chair, apparently totally relaxed in the knowledge of the saintly protection he has just acquired. There is nothing for me to do but to accept defeat graciously and return to filling the bowls and passing them to Francis, who then passes them on until everyone has soup. The breadbasket is similarly shared, and there is nothing for me to do but relax and join in the eating and conversation.

"This is certainly delicious," says Hildegard, after several spoonfuls. "It reminds me very much of a soup Jutta would make for me when, as a child, I was first sent into her care."

"Oh, I would very much like to hear about your early years, Hildegard. Please tell us," urges Margery.

"Very well," agrees Hildegard, putting down the spoon to take up her glass for a sip of wine before beginning. "Of course, it was a very long time ago. And while I remember Jutta's soup with clarity, many other aspects of my childhood are blurred in my memory, almost dreamlike. However, I can say that I was born in the year 1098 in Bermersheim, not far from modern-day Mainz in the German Rhineland. My parents were of noble stock and, in comparison to many others, we were a well-to-do family. Some say I was my parents' tenth child and, as such, was destined to be tithed to the Church. It may have been so, but I cannot be sure because children then often died in infancy, making the counting of offspring subjective for all but the poor mother who, no doubt, held each birth—alive or dead—deeply in her heart. One of my hagiographers, Godfrey of Disibodenberg, wrote that I displayed such remarkable holiness from a very young age that my parents knew they had to pledge me to religious life. Childish ignorance as well as humility prevent me from confirming or denying both the tithing theory and the opinion of my piety as the prompts for my parents' action but, in any event, I was given to the Church at about seven years of age. The first stage of this dedication took me into the care of the anchoress Jutta for my basic education and instruction in the religious life.

"Excuse me, Hildegard," I say, reluctant to break the flow of her story, "but could you explain what an anchoress is?"

"I could. But as the anchoresses of the Rhineland of the twelfth century differ in many ways from the larger number of dedicated anchoresses that flourished a century or two later in England, and as we are privileged to have with us one of the greatest and most famous anchoresses of all times, I would like to ask her to give an account of the vocation." Hildegard looks across the table at Julian. "Would you be so kind, Julian?"

"Gladly, dear Hildegard. So long as you promise to return to the story of your childhood when I have completed my description."

Hildegard smiles and nods in Julian's direction and, seeming to be grateful for the shift in attention, she returns in earnest to her soup and bread.

Julian, moves her bowl to one side, sits up very straight in her chair and looks at each guest in acknowledgment before beginning, "Anchoresses were a particular feature of religious dedication and practice in medieval England. There were men, too, who took up this way of life and they were known as 'anchorites.' Here, I must acknowledge that I know and appreciate that, in this present time, such gendered language is not used, but it was the way of things in the medieval era and, thus, I want to be clear in the information I am about to give you. You see, there were some differences in the manner in which men and women lived the life and, as you will appreciate, I can only speak reliably of the female experience. So, anchoresses were women whose love of God propelled them to seek an extreme form of solitary life whereby they became willingly enclosed, for life, in a small cell called an 'anchorhold,' usually attached to a church. There they pursued a life of prayer and contemplation. Those seeking enclosure usually required funds of their own, or some form of reliable sponsorship from a well-to-do individual, to embark on the life, but after enclosure they were maintained, at least in part, by people of the town or parish. At all times, anchoresses were under the supervision of the local bishop and subject to Church rules and a nominated spiritual director. As you would understand, it was a solemn vocation, and this was highlighted by each enclosure being preceded by a Mass for the Dead. The significance of this was that the woman being enclosed—and, indeed, all who looked on—understood that the anchoress was dead to the world but alive to Christ. You might further understand that the anchoritic life was rarely the life choice of a very young woman and that those responding to this call had usually discerned their solitary vocation over some years, many of the women proceeding to it after living, for a time, the communal religious life of a nun in the convent."

"I'm amazed to hear such a vocation existed. Such dedication," I say, my amazement matched only by my curiosity. "What was life like—your life in particular—inside an anchorhold, Julian?"

"Well, for me, it was a good life; the only one I desired to lead after I received my insights. As a young girl, I had not envisaged becoming an anchoress, although I was very devoted to my prayers; and I had a great love of God and the Church. Later, however, when circumstances changed and the call to the solitary life of an anchoress captured my soul, I gladly embraced it. My admittance to the anchorhold was the same as I have just described for all anchoresses: a Mass for the Dead after which I was led by the bishop to be locked permanently into my cell which was attached to the Church of St. Julian's in Carrow, Norwich. There I . . ."

"Pardon my interruption, Julian," I say, "but I've read that 'Julian' was the name you took on entering the anchorhold at St. Julian's Church. Is that correct?"

"Yes, it is so, dear Annie. Not a coincidence at all, as some have suggested. 'Julian' was not my given name. Rather, I assumed the name of the church of my enclosure as a mark of respect for the blessing that was being bestowed upon me, and because I was happy to signal, in my change of name, that I was leaving behind my old life."

It is on the tip of my tongue to ask Julian what her birth name was when, out of the corner of my eye, I catch Hildegard's stern shake of the head which leaves me in no doubt that, first, she knows exactly what I'm thinking of asking and, secondly, the asking of it would be inappropriate. I take the abbess's hint and ask Julian to go on with the account of her life in the anchorhold.

Julian obliges and continues, "My anchorhold, like so many others, was small—about twelve feet by twelve feet—and had a floor of packed earth. There was a small fireplace which I greatly appreciated, as my cell was built onto the north side of the church, next to the graveyard. This siting of the cell adjacent to the graveyard was common and served as a further reminder to the anchoress that she was dead to the world but alive spiritually. On one side of the fireplace was a simple wooden altar on which sat two tallow candles in holders, and my two books—a Bible and a rule for anchoresses. On the other side, in the corner against one wall, I had a pallet bed with a thin straw mattress and a coarse woolen blanket. At the foot of the bed was a small chest for storing a change of clothes and an extra shawl. A tiny trestle table and a wooden chair completed the furnishings. There were windows: one, often called the 'squint,' that opened into the church, and through this window I received my spiritual nourishment of the Eucharist; another window, next to the permanently locked door through which I had entered my cell, opened onto a small ante-room for my serving maid, a kind and dedicated helper who brought me my food and who, even more kindly, was responsible for removing the day and night waste from my cell; and then there was a third 'public' window, always covered by a heavy oiled cloth, even when its shutters were opened. This window served an important function because, as you know, the parish church, to which cells like mine were attached, were usually at the center of the town and therefore always busy with people. And, on certain days of the week, I would take time to honor God through the practice of being present for my fellow Christians when they came to my public window to ask for my prayers, and sometimes my advice on problems and worries in their lives. In this way, I was a conduit for God's counsel as well as a living sign of piety within their midst."

Margery, waving a hand in Julian's direction to catch her attention, says, "Yes, yes. And I was one of those visitors to Julian's anchorhold window. Do you remember, Julian?"

"Of course, I remember, Margery. I believe it was in the year 1413 or thereabouts."

"Yes, exactly," confirms Margery, and then, darting her eyes around the table, she continues, "Julian was well known in her own lifetime as a holy woman, you know, so I was very keen to visit her. Do you recall our conversation, Julian?"

"Most definitely. But why don't you share the details with our friends here, Margery?"

"Oh, I'd love to. Yes, as Julian has said, it was around the year 1413 that I took myself to Norwich, seeking encouragement and validation for the manner of life I was pursuing in my efforts to honor the many great gifts and insights our dear Lord had bestowed on me."

"Why did you need validation, Margery?" Francis asks.

"It is a fair question, Francis. And one that I can answer only by telling something of my story and the way in which God stirred my soul. But I am aware that we still have much to hear of Hildegard's and Julian's stories." Margery glances at Hildegard and then Julian, as if seeking permission to proceed.

"For my part, please go ahead, Margery," says Hildegard, turning the palm of her right hand up in a gesture that indicates assent. "You shall hear more about me in due course."

"Likewise," smiles Julian. "There is time for all."

Margery beams. "Well, best to begin at the beginning then," she announces, leaning back in the chair and resting her interlaced fingers atop her ample girth. "I was born in 1373, in England, in the Norfolk town of Bishop's Lynn[2]

---

2. Today, Bishop's Lynn is known as King's Lynn, the name change coming about in the sixteenth century after the dissolution of the monasteries by King Henry VIII.

where my father, John Brunham, was mayor for five separate terms. When I was twenty, I married John Kempe, an honorable burgess of the town and, as nature intends, within a year of our marriage, I gave birth to our first child. I went on to have thirteen more children, but this first birth was especially difficult, and afterwards I was no longer the same woman I had once been; I was much distressed, to the point that I thought of harming myself. You, perhaps, would react in a similar way if you were tormented by devils for half a year or more."

"Oh, Margery! We *do* understand such distress now," I offer. "We would call it post-partum depression or even post-partum psychosis."

Margery shoots an alarmed look at me. "No, I don't think so, dear Annie. It was my own failure to confess a great sin that brought such anguish upon me. But God is merciful and, after a time, it was God, in the person of Jesus himself, who appeared to me and restored my health."

I decide it is best not to contradict Margery, and instead sit quietly, reflecting on the way in which, to our modern sensibilities, any visions—menacing or marvelous—are considered to be indicative of mental illness. Margery herself, I realize, though laid low by the terrifying and devilish visions, is focusing on her return to good health brought about by her vision of Jesus. I turn my attention back to her story.

"With my strength restored, I was eager to resume my previously active life in the commercial and social activities of the town. But what do you think? The brewing enterprise that I pursued suddenly went awry. The beer went flat, and nothing I tried could produce a froth. Not one bubble. And so I turned my mercantile hand to milling, engaging a strong laborer and purchasing two sturdy horses to grind local people's corn for a tidy profit—or so I thought. Until, without reason or cause, the horses refused to pull. Again, my business failed. And thus I had to face the fact that my failures were due to my disregard of the spiritual privilege I'd received when Jesus appeared to me. I had continued with my life of covetousness, vanity, and love of fashionable clothes, putting all this ahead of God's will." Margery pauses and pulls a handkerchief out of one of her sleeves to dab at the tears welling in her eyes.

"You were not to know, Margery," says Cloud. "We humans take a long time to come to true self-knowledge. Remember, you had been born into a mercantile family and would have felt some responsibility toward that way of life. And you were a wife and mother."

"Thank you for the reassurance, Cloud. You do touch on something of the conflict I was experiencing at the time. But I cannot deny that in the depths of my soul, I knew God was calling me. I knew I had to change my ways, and so I begged for mercy. Soon after, my dear Lord responded by awakening me in the middle of the night with an audition—some call it an auditory revelation—of the most melodious sounds. I knew that I was being given an auditory 'preview' of the bliss of heaven."

"I, too, have heard such melodies, Margery," offers Richard. "Sounds so rare that I could not deny their divine origin."

All eyes shift to Richard, but he waves away our attention, promising that he will say more about this later in the meal. "Please, go on with your story now, Margery," he urges.

Margery doesn't need to be told twice and, tucking the handkerchief back into her sleeve, she continues, "After that,

I redirected my life's efforts accordingly. No longer would I seek success and recognition in the material world but, instead, only in the realm of the spiritual. From that moment, I threw herself into a mode of life that I thought fittingly reflected the honor I had received. Most obviously, I prayed. A lot! I would arise at two or three in the morning and make my way to church where I would pray until midday and then again in the later afternoon. I confessed to a priest twice and, sometimes, three times a day, seeking, in particular, forgiveness for that early sin I had avoided confessing for many years. I adopted stringent fasting and the wearing of a hair shirt made from the coarse cloth on which malt was dried. And, much to my husband's chagrin, I attempted to live chastely in our married situation by avoiding all sexual contact with him."

"Oh, Margery, such extremes," I cannot help but say.

"You are correct, Annie. I never could do things by half. In no small part, I was my own worst enemy. In truth, my efforts in many areas of my new spiritual life were not entirely successful. Some in the community said my enthusiastic praying and extremes of mortification were not sincere but, rather, all for show. And I did bear fourteen children in total to my dear husband, so many doubted my commitment to living chastely within marriage and, in that regard, others ridiculed me for the wearing of white clothes that represented chastity, but I wanted to wear them more as a sign of my intention, my hope, of chastity. All this doubt and derision around me became the reason that I sought validation for my mystical experiences, and my way of life." Margery grins, explaining, "Now, Francis, you see, with this circuitous account, I have finally answered your question. I needed validation because there was a great chasm between my inner experience of deep spirituality and my outer way of life as a wife and prominent townswoman."

"You make a valid point, Margery." Hildegard is nodding sagely. "You were in a precarious position for a woman; very different from the position Julian and I were in. We were under the auspices of the official Church and, therefore, automatically validated within our communities. I was a Benedictine nun, an abbess, and Julian was a professed anchoress. Thus, to the observer, our inner and outer lives were aligned —at least in theory. I add this qualification because, although we were supported and sanctioned by the Church, we were, as women, also subject to Church control. And then, even more so than now, that meant 'male' control. Of course, as we know, we are all equal in God's eyes, and it was not appropriate for me—nor for Julian, I'm sure—to mindlessly 'toe the line,' as they say in the modern idiom, when God had planned greater things for us, insofar as we were made instruments of the Divine's great works. But you, Margery, were a secular woman, out and about in the community, not subject to the rules and the protection of a religious profession, nor to male oversight. You were a woman with your own ideas and, it seems, a kind husband, who was too devoted to you to demand absolute obedience from you. In short, Margery, you were dangerous. And I mean that as a compliment!"

Francis claps his hands. "Yes, you made people think differently about things. That is following Jesus's example. Speaking truth to power. You did it, too, Hildegard. And Julian. All of you shook things up."

"Don't leave yourself out of that group, Francis," Richard says. "You, especially, reminded the Church of its need to really follow the gospel message, to value poverty of spirit over any and all material wealth, to care for the poor, to respond to God's call. Why, you went all the way to Rome and pestered the pope until he approved your new order of friars. And we still have the Franciscans today."

Francis bows his head in humble thanks at Richard's words, but it is Margery who replies, "I am honored to be included in such company, but I must add that I didn't feel dangerous or empowered. Most of the time I was very frightened, and very unsure. You know, in the early years of my new spiritual life, I received from God the 'gift of tears.' Now, some I conferred with assured me that this was a special gift, but I suffered sorely because of it."

"I, too, received the gift of tears," murmurs Francis. "For me, it was a sweet affliction, but not easy. And I was in a very different situation from you, Margery."

The table is silent for a moment, waiting for Francis to continue. But, again, he bows his head, making it clear that he will say no more on the subject at present.

"Can you say a little more about your experience of this gift, Margery?" I ask.

"Well, I knew it was God-given but it was, as Francis has said, not easy. It was unsought and unpredictable. I would find myself crying and even wailing in response to particular things. The mere mention of the name 'Jesus,' or the sight of a small boy with his mother, for example, might send me into uncontrollable sobs. Some priests refused to allow me in the church when they were to preach, lest I wail at their utterance of the holy name. Even in the medieval period, such conduct was unacceptable to most people, and I found myself often shunned by those who had witnessed my behavior. I grant you that this and, as I've already said, my various self-imposed mortifications, were a little extreme, but I had to follow the stirrings of my soul. Despite trying to live out my convictions with courage, the ridicule that was frequently heaped upon me confused me, simultaneously fortifying and weakening my resolve. In other words, the condemnation leveled at me and the ostracism I endured as a result of it served in one way as a reinforcement of the fact that I was suffering in pale reflection of Jesus's own suffering; in another way, I saw my own self-doubt mirrored and magnified by many of those around me, and that set me on a course of self-validation, of seeking assurance from a great array of religious and civil authorities. Yes, perhaps my faith was insufficient but, at times, I worried terribly about being in error. I wanted only to give honor to God and was grateful for those who supported me, seeing the truth of my piety. This led me to pursue audiences with many of the most influential personages of my day, one of these being our dear friend here, Julian of Norwich. And so there remains only one very important thing for me to say before I bring this part of my story to a close so that others may speak. And that is that I told Julian of my spiritual experiences, of the graces of compunction, contrition, compassion, sweetness, and devotion, and the wonderful revelations that our dear Lord had granted me, and I begged her to tell me if she discerned any error in anything I was describing because, even then, Julian was known to be of exceptional wisdom in such things, and a woman of unfailingly good counsel."

"And what was your insight, Julian?" Richard inquires.

"Quite simply that all Margery had told me was compatible with the work of the Holy Spirit, that all she was experiencing were signs of God's great love for us. I urged her to persevere and assured her of my prayers of support."

"Hear, hear," says Richard, raising his wine glass as we all follow suit, joining in the acclamation.

"Julian was so gracious. You can't know how much that meant to me, to have your encouragement. Thank you," Margery raises her glass in specific salute to Julian.

Julian smiles in acknowledgment but, in her quiet and humble way, she deflects attention from herself by suggesting that Hildegard resume her story.

"Very glad to do so, Julian," Hildegard nods, "but, Richard, perhaps you will be kind enough to furnish me with a little more wine before I begin."

Richard stands and walks around the table, topping up everyone's beverage as required.

Hildegard takes a good sip of the refreshed drink and closes her eyes for a moment, as if in thought, before commencing. "Now, where was I? . . . On my way to Jutta's anchorhold, I believe. Ah, I vividly remember that morning when I left my parents' home. Permit me a poetic reverie on the topic, if you will. Not from my writings, something that just came to me, especially for this dinner."

An unusual stillness suddenly envelops our group and, following Hildegard's lead, we close our eyes as we listen to her words:

> *I see myself as a small child, clever, precocious, being*
> *led by my father. It was a frosty morning, the*
> *light pale through the woodland.*
> *A bird on a low branch, piping piteously in the ap-*
> *proaching winter.*
> *A gust, the bird is shaken, uplifts itself on startled*
> *wings, and lets a feather flutter downward.*

*It hovers in its descent, and I, breathing out a
   hoary breath, try to send it back, skyward.*
*The breath and feather coalesce, and I am that
   breath, and I am that feather.*
A feather on the breath of God.
*Still morning, still frosty, I arrive at Jutta's an-
   chorhold,*
And there I'm held gently for my education.
Do you see the young girl? Eager. Enraptured.

In my imagination I do see the young girl and her father, I feel the chill approach of winter, I hear the bird, I watch the delicate feather, and I grasp, so fleetingly and so beyond explanation, something of Hildegard's mystical calling.

I sense that all of our little group is similarly entranced until Hildegard abruptly puts the poetry aside as she continues, "From Jutta, I would receive a basic education and instruction in the religious life. Jutta's piety, however, saw her attract more young girls for instruction and, while I was still a teenager, Jutta's cell could no longer accommodate all her young charges, and the cell's occupants were transferred to re-establish as a small Benedictine convent. I was happy with the change in circumstances and thrived in the new conventual environment and, when Jutta died in 1136, I was elected to the position of abbess, assuming leadership of the convent. Sometime after this, in 1141, the visions that had been with me since childhood intensified, and when, for various reasons, they were brought to the attention of Pope Eugenius, he sent instructions that I was to record them in detail. Thus began my lifelong writing career and the production of a very wide range of works, some details of which, I think, might be of interest to you later in our meal this evening."

"Your description of the receipt of your visions strikes such a chord with me," comments Francis.

"Please tell us, Francis," Hildegard urges.

"I am happy to say something of myself but, like Margery, and unlike you, Hildegard, my spiritual life came to fruition when I was an adult. It was a huge change for me, so, if you will bear with me, I shall say something of my early life too, as a point of contrast to my later life, in order to illustrate God's workings in my soul."

Of course there is unanimous agreement, and attention is quickly riveted on Francis.

"I was born around 1181 in Assisi in Umbria. My father, Pietro di Bernadone, was a wealthy cloth merchant. I have been told that while my father was away, my mother, Pica, had me christened 'Giovanni,' but that my father, on his return, renamed me 'Francis,' because he had a great fondness for France, and carried out much of his business there. In my younger years I enjoyed the life that my father's wealth afforded me but, at the same time, I longed for adventure and, when the opportunity arose, I eagerly took part in one of the region's civil wars between 1201 and 1202. I was not quite the knight I imagined myself to be and, at the battle of Collestrada, which the Assisi forces lost, I was captured, and I spent a year in prison until I was ransomed by my rich father. Once released and back in Assisi, I worked, somewhat reluctantly, for my father while continuing my life of feasting and womanizing.

"And soon, still longing for adventure, I decided to enlist in the army of Count Walter of Brienne with the aim of journeying with him and his men to fight in the Fourth Crusade. En route to southern Italy, however, I began to experience strange dreams and visions and I knew I had to return to Assisi. On my homecoming, I was met with derision from my father and his friends for my apparent failure of courage. By then, however, the idea of working in my father's cloth shop by day and participating in lavish feasts and entertainments by night filled me with dread. In fact, sometime around 1205, I began to avoid all my former companions, preferring instead to wander alone on the hillside to deserted places outside the town. I was drawn, too, to the leper house outside Assisi, and there I began to nurse the sick. Then one day, late in 1205, my wanderings took me to the old church of San Damiano, where I stood in front of a Byzantine crucifix with the figure of Christ upon it. As I gazed on it, the figure of Christ became vivified. Yes, it came to life and Christ spoke to me, instructing me to repair the church. At the time, I did not appreciate the full extent of Christ's words but his living, suffering body elicited a profound change in me, nonetheless."

Francis pauses, his bright eyes staring ahead. All at the table are quiet, except for their breathing which seems to be synchronized. It is Julian who breaks the silence, saying, "I am very moved to hear you speak of this experience with the crucifix, because I, too, was precipitated into God's exquisite revelations of divine love by witnessing, suddenly and unbidden, the Christ figure on the cross coming to life." She lowers her head.

"Please, tell us of this introduction to your visions," encourages Cloud.

"Yes, all the details, please," says Margery.

When Julian lifts her face, it seems as if she is looking at something far beyond this dining room and this moment in time. She replies, "Gladly, if you so wish. Actually, it began on a bright day in May 1373, in the bustling port town of

Norwich in the east of England. I see it clearly. I am thirty and a half years old, and I am gravely ill. My dear mother, thinking it unlikely that her beloved daughter will survive, summons the priest to administer the last rites. Eventually he arrives and begins his duties by placing a crucifix at the foot of the bed, in clear line of my now failing eyesight. The priest and my mother and others in attendance at the bedside continue to busy themselves with the preparation and implementation of the important end-of-life ritual. Somber and reverent, they know it is necessary to prepare a dying person's soul for its imminent release back to its Creator. Fragrant oils are placed on a small table, candles are lit, and quiet incantations are begun. All who are there see, hear, smell, and touch the accoutrements of departure from life. All except me. I see only the crucifix in front of me; more precisely, I see the body on the crucifix: the living, suffering, bleeding, agonized body of my savior. As the room around me darkens, a beam of glowing light focuses itself on the crown of thorns on my Lord's head. From under the encircling thorns, his blood flows copiously, in great drops. My sight follows the movement of the drops down his face and onto his chest. My breath shortens and my pain increases, and I feel certain that I am at the point of death, but there is nothing that can coax my eyes away from my Lord Jesus. And then, without averting my eyes, my mind is suddenly taken to a time in my childhood when I had prayed for three graces from God. And the first of these, so clear in my recollection, was for a vivid experience— a bodily sight as it were—of Christ's passion. And I realize that, here, in front of me, is the very grace I had desired. And then, the second grace for which I had longed also came to mind; and it was the desire for a bodily sickness, so severe that I might die. And here, again, I am aware that I am receiving my desire. Next, my mind simultaneously wondered and knew that the third grace—a desire for the three wounds of contrition, compassion, and the unfettered longing for and aligning of my will with God's—would also be granted. And though, in all these desires, I had never thought of, nor requested, visions and revelations, yet here, in this room, in the suffering body of Christ on the Cross, was the fulfillment of all my prayers, and more. From this point, I entered into a mystical state in which I was to be the recipient of sixteen extraordinary revelations of God's love. Suddenly, the world as I had known it in my thirty years of life changes, is transformed into something new."

Julian finishes speaking, but the scene she has conjured lingers before my eyes. I long to hear more, but I also sense that my guests are carefully, and deliberately, pacing the conversation. That is, I suspect that, really, they are talking about their own beginnings in the mystical life, and that more details about what follows in those lives will be discussed when the time is right.

As if confirming my intuition, Hildegard breaks the stillness of the circle by leaning forward to rest her elbows on the table and confiding, "I, too, was propelled into my visions by way of an illness. Blinding headaches, actually.... Hard to explain, but I know they were divinely inspired, despite what modern-day neurologists say, preferring to diagnose 'migraine' as if that were the end of it instead of looking further and realizing that it was the beginning, the means to all that followed. God can do all things, but how blessed we are that God usually brings the miraculous to our attention via ordinary, natural things. And what is more ordinary than a headache? By the grace of those headaches, God showed me all things. Permit me, if you will, another poetic explanation which, again, though you will not find it in any of my writings, is an apt summary:

I am a seer, seared by God in the fiery furnace of
*   far-seeing Love.*
A burning pain, flashing specks of light before my
*   eyes.*
They hover in their ascent, and I, breathing out
*   with painéd breath, try to expel them, skyward.*
The fire and the pain coalesce
And God is the light,
And I am the phoenix,
God's own phoenix, forged in fire,
Frightened, enlightened. Engulfed in God's love.

Hildegard settles back in her chair, and we know that she has said all that she wants to say for the moment.

Cloud now leans forward to rest his elbows on the table and, bringing his hands together in a prayer-like pose, he taps his index fingers to his lips briefly before sweeping his gaze around the table and saying, "Margery, you have told us that you entered your mystical life by way of illness. Francis, you have shared how you were brought low by mental and emotional anguish. Julian and Hildegard, you too were cast down in illness before being lifted up to see beyond life's veil. It seems to me that, often, the eternal God breaks through into the everyday when our physical and mental reserves are depleted. Thank you all for sharing these commonalities, these harmonies, in your experience."

There is quiet agreement, and chatting between those guests seated next to each other takes over from the group discussion. As if registering the change in the dynamic of the conversation, even Pat the dog stretches under Francis's chair and lets out a loud exhalation. This is my cue to clear away the empty soup bowls. I decline offers of assistance with a shake of my head and carry the gathered bowls to the kitchen. A quick rinse and they're in the dishwasher. Next, I take the salad greens and quartered figs out of the fridge but leave them covered on the counter while, in a pan on the stove, I quickly toast some sesame seeds to sprinkle over the salad. As they're turning golden, I mix honey and balsamic vinegar, ready to dress the salad before serving. Then I turn to the fridge again to take out the salmon fillets, already arranged on a roasting tray. I season them simply with salt and pepper and lemon slices and a splash of olive oil, and cover the tray with some foil before placing it onto the upper shelf of the oven. On the lower shelf, and just needing to be heated through, I place the large, covered dish of baked barley with spinach and mushrooms that I'd prepared earlier. I set the timer for twenty minutes and, mentally checking that my preparations for the main course are all in place, I hurry back to the dining room, fretting that I might be missing something important in the conversation.

Smiling faces turn to me as I enter. "Come, sit, and relax! We don't want you working too hard for us this evening," says Richard, as he comes to pull my chair out for me.

"Thank you, Richard. No need to worry. It's a very simple meal tonight, really. Just the usual last minute things to do. But before I sit, can I refill your glasses?"

"Already done," laughs Francis. "We have had many years of managing all kinds of things for ourselves."

"Well then, on that topic, more or less, could you tell us what happened, Francis, after your experience in the church at San Damiano?" I ask.

"It would be my humble pleasure," Francis responds. "When God had asked me to repair the church, I took it as a divine directive to rebuild the crumbling church of San Damiano stone by stone, and I lost no time in setting to work. Materials for such a renovation, of course, were costly, and I managed to pay for the more urgent repairs only by selling one of my father's horses and a bale of his most expensive cloth. Perhaps understandably, my father was disappointed in the work that I was pursuing and, perhaps even more understandably, infuriated by my use of his property to fund the work. He told me that he thought I was crazy and that the only way to bring me under control and back to my senses was by bringing charges against me, in front of the town council. What was I to do? It was hard to disappoint my father, but impossible to disregard God's request. And so, a little creative tableau for you, just as I remember it:

An October morning in the year 1206. The piazza of Assisi is alive with activity, electric with curiosity. The crowd presses in as a young man, the son of a good mercantile family, makes his way to the center of the piazza and composes himself to stand still and straight, with his gaze steady but focused nowhere in particular, even when the charges of the community are levelled at him.

"Francis, son of Pietro di Bernadone," they cry, "you have taken money from your father and used it, without his permission, toward the purchase of materials to rebuild an old church. In addition, you have sold cloth from your father's shop for the same purpose and yet, all the while, you have had no hesitation in wearing cloth from the same source as your own apparel. How do you respond?" The young man responds by

stripping himself bare, right there in the town square, and handing the clothing to his father. "Henceforth," he declares, "I will turn to God and call him my father in heaven."

Francis's story ends abruptly, and he hangs his head.

"Oh Francis. How sad for you, for your father, and for your community, that they did not understand. And yet, how authentic. And necessary...in being true to God's call, I mean. I can empathize completely," says Margery.

"Yes, such a difficult time for you," reflects Richard. "But I, too, can understand, having also rejected my previous life. And having also taken on, let's say, a drastic change in clothes."

"Intriguing, Richard. Please tell us more. Tell us something of your own entry into the mystical life," encourages Francis, and Richard readily obliges.

"Mine was a call that crept up on me, at first, and then became overwhelming. I was born in the year 1300, or thereabouts, into a farming family in the area of Thornton-le-Dale, Yorkshire, in the north of England. I was a bright child and, after I had performed well in the early years of my education, the archdeacon of Durham, Thomas Neville, sponsored me to attend Oxford University. While there, although I was fascinated by the study of theology, something deeper was also stirring in me and, to the disappointment of many, I abandoned my studies before completing my master's because I felt called, instead, to the life of a hermit." Here Richard pauses and shoots me a glance. It is as if he has read my mind when he asks, "Annie, would you like me to briefly explain the difference between an anchorite and a hermit?"

I nod.

"I thought so," Richard acknowledges. "Well then, on one level, according to their motivation and purpose, the two vocations are similar in that both the anchorite and the hermit seek a retirement from the world in order to live a solitary life devoted to prayer. It is on the practical level that they differ, with the anchorite, on the one hand, being of fixed abode—that is, living the whole of his life in a small, locked cell and under the auspices and direction of the bishop and the local parish—in a public part of a village or town. The hermit, on the other hand, makes his home in any number of available dwelling places, such as caves or abandoned cottages, and in geographically diverse and widespread locations. The anchorite, enclosed as he is, is dependent upon others for his sustenance and general upkeep; but the hermit is entirely self-sufficient, self-directed, and self-supporting, often maintaining himself by providing a community service such as assisting travelers across a stream, or providing refreshment for travelers, in exchange for small amounts of money or provisions. I might add that, by the medieval period, female hermits were frowned upon in England because the commonly-held view was that women could not be self-directing or self-supporting but, instead, should always be under male supervision if they wanted to pursue a solitary life. And thus, as a matter of interest, there was a burgeoning in the number of anchoresses at that time, because it became the only option for those women who desired a solitary life of prayer and contemplation."

"Thank you, Richard. Such a clear explanation of the differences," I say. "And you were kind to interrupt your own story to clarify that for me, so now please take up the account of your entry into the hermit life."

"Ah, ha," he laughs. "My entry into the life of a hermit was dramatic, to say the least. Sometime after leaving Oxford, I was residing in my father's house and, though I had set my intention on becoming a hermit, on this particular day the urge to change my life, to give up everything I had pursued and represented to this point, was overwhelming. And so I asked my dear sister if I could have two of her tunics and, in addition, that she might bring me my father's rain hood. She agreed and, when I received these items from her, I set about cutting and refashioning the garments into my own version of a religious habit. As Francis has described doing in the piazza in Assisi, I also stripped off my old clothes and donned my new apparel and then felt ready to assume my hermitic lifestyle."

"Putting off the old and putting on the new, as it says in Ephesians," says Hildegard. "A powerful symbol of change."

"Yes," agrees Richard. "I felt the need to signal my change of focus—from the material to the spiritual—to my community and family as well as to myself. It is what Margery spoke of earlier—the need to make apparent the inward change by a very obvious outward change.

"It's no coincidence that religiously professed people have, for centuries, discarded the clothing of their society and taken up the wearing of a habit," says Cloud. "In the language of what is now called 'Middle English,' the word 'habit' had the threefold connotation of a type of religious attire, a customary practice, and one's bodily and mental constitution. From there, it is easy to understand how leaving the everyday world to take on the religious or contemplative life, was a change of habit in all three modes, clothing being the most obvious. I understand that, even in this twenty-first century, the connection between outer clothes and inner disposition is strong. For example, I have noticed that if someone now feels down, they might decide to change, improve, their outer appearance by losing weight, buying a new outfit, getting a new hairstyle, and so on.

"What you are saying is of great interest to me," says Margery. "As you've noted, and I had already begun to explain, I came to a point where I felt it was necessary to change my outward appearance, my clothing, to match my inner awakening. But for me, as I mentioned, the change was not well received by my community. On reflection, perhaps those who were against me in this may have had a point. I sought to wear white clothing as a sign of my 'virginity' in Christ. Obviously, as a mother who had given birth to fourteen children, I was not a virgin in the usual, physical sense and, further, perhaps I was stepping on the toes, so to speak, of those who wore white clothing as a legitimate sign of their religious profession. In retrospect, then, I can look more kindly on those who ridiculed me. Still, it seemed such an important thing for me to do at the time, and your explanation, dear Cloud, has validated my motivation, putting it into perspective for me."

Cloud nods his head. "Your perspective is sound on this, Margery. And I think you and Richard and Francis were responding to something very deep in our medieval way of seeing things. In the Middle Ages, even more than now, we judged people by their clothes. Those of the upper class had the means to indulge in intricately designed clothes fashioned from beautiful fabrics; the poor had no choice and were instantly recognizable, and easily dismissed, in their coverings of rags."

"Precisely," agrees Francis. "After I rejected all that my earthly father represented, I began to dress in rags, to align my inner devotion to a poverty of the spirit and my outward appearance. And once I had made that change of clothing, other things that I needed to do became clearer too. I fraternized with the poor and the sick and devoted my time to repairing, in addition to San Damiano, other ruined chapels and churches in the countryside around Assisi—among them, the Porziuncola, a small chapel now within the Basilica of St. Mary of the Angels, which, as you might know, was to become the center of our new order of friars. But I am jumping ahead here. Back to our topic of clothes and lifestyle, I lived alone in my rags, continuing to work on repairing what I could as I wandered the hills until one day in February 1209, I heard, as if anew, the Gospel of Matthew: 'Take no gold, or silver or copper in your belts, no bag for your journey, or two tunics, or sandals, or a staff; for the laborers deserve their food. Whatever town or village you enter, find out who in it is worthy, and stay there until you leave' (Matt 10:9–12). It struck such a deep chord with me that I was drawn to change again, this time from my solitary life to that of a mendicant preacher, that is, one who travels around preaching and living only on what he can beg from others. And soon, God's grace encouraged other men to join me. Some had been very wealthy men, but they, too, took the gospel message to heart and changed their habits in every way and followed me, a lowly man, who was following in the steps of the example of Jesus Christ."

Hildegard claps her hands. "Well said, and well done, Francis. Yes, you were following Jesus but your change was still a courageous one, albeit no doubt seemingly strange to those of later times. Let me remind you all that the twelfth and thirteenth centuries were strange times in many ways, and the religious situation, in particular, was one of change and foment. Certainly, the monastic movement—the monks in their monasteries, and the nuns in their convents, following the ancient Rule of St. Benedict—had prayed and worked and invented hospitality and faithfully copied the sacred texts and contributed hugely to the development of Western civilization, but even great institutions can become stale, even corrupt; and Francis, and men and women like him, were called on to renew that which was crumbling for lack of proper attention and maintenance, and to breathe fresh air into stagnant places."

"Much was changing then, wasn't it?" I contribute. "From my reading, I know that the landscape of the medieval cities was transformed as magnificent Gothic cathedrals arose and pushed into the skies. And the people, reading the stories of the Bible and Church tradition in the images of the cathedrals' stained glass windows, started to feel the change in the air. All sorts of men were taking the Gospel to the people in the streets and the countryside. Many were unauthorized—unauthorized by the Church, I mean. And all sorts of men—and, horror of horrors, even women—were gathering to listen to the preaching in the streets and countryside. And the preaching of those gospel stories was being relayed *not* in Latin but in people's own vernacular. And the Church decreed that much of this unauthorized preaching was heresy. The Church's authority was really being threatened, wasn't it?"

"Exactly," agrees Francis. "And can you imagine Pope Innocent III's shock when, adding to the disjuncture of the times, I went with eleven spiritual brothers all the way to Rome to seek papal approval of a new religious order based on poverty? No property, therefore no friary. Just groups of dedicated men, out and about among the people, preaching God's word, truly following the example of Jesus's life. It was no surprise that the pope was reluctant to even admit to his presence such a scruffy band, let alone give his approval to the new enterprise we were proposing. We were faced with flat denial until, again by God's good grace, the pope had a dream in which he saw me literally propping up a crumbling church edifice. How humbled I was to realize that God's initial message to me—to rebuild the church, and which, in my ignorance, I had taken to mean that I should rebuild the church of San Damiano where I received God's instruction— was actually a call for me and my brothers to renew, with God's love, the whole institution of the Church. By means of the dream, God got the message through to the pope too, and on April 16, 1210, we received oral approval for the Rule that I, Francis, had set out for our little group, and we were officially given the name of the 'Order of Friars Minor' (the Lesser Brothers). Our charter, our main rule of life, was to preach the Gospel on the streets to all and to have no possessions, to exist in absolute poverty. And, of course, with the papal approval, more men joined and our little order grew and grew."

"There is no question that it was providential that your order was approved, Francis. Sorely needed by the Church at that time," observes Hildegard. "For me, however, and for my nuns—being women, and already within the Benedictine order under the oversight and guidance of the Church—though we saw many aspects of the Church that were in need of reform and renewal, we had to proceed more subtly. That is not to say that I did not seek a renewal of the life of dedicated prayer and work for my nuns. In fact, the opposite is true, and it brought me into conflict with the male authorities on occasions. For example, at one point, it became obvious that the nuns needed a return to a simpler and more prayerful and less distracted environment and, therefore, as abbess, I pushed for this and found myself at odds with the Benedictine (male) house that had jurisdiction over us. Specifically, I petitioned Abbot Kuno for permission to move my nuns away from Disibodenberg and his oversight and to establish a more austere convent at Rupertsberg. Kuno's strident disapproval forced me to seek approval from the archbishop. Under such pressure, Kuno finally relented and, in 1150, twenty nuns and my confessor, secretary and scribe, Volmar, headed for Rupertsberg. But, enough of this. Further details of my own experiences are, I think, conversations best left for later in the evening." Hildegard brings her lips together with exaggerated firmness to underline her point.

No one disagrees, and a brief moment of thoughtful silence ensues. My mind turns to something I've been observing throughout the course of the meal, and that is that while Cloud has contributed to the conversation on pertinent points, he has said virtually nothing about his own entrance into the mystical life. And, apparently, I am not the only one who has noticed this because the moment's silence is broken when Margery asks, "Dear Cloud . . . what of your life?"

"Ah, a good question. Well, I have been variously described as a secular priest, a monk, a Carthusian, not a Carthusian, a hermit, a recluse, and a country parson, but the truth is that my back story is not...ah...ah....Perhaps I could tell you about...."

Beep, beep, beep. The intense focus on what Cloud is about to reveal is split by the oven timer shrieking its coded message that the fish is cooked.

"Oh, so sorry, Cloud. Please, go on. The fish can wait a little longer," I say.

"No," declares Cloud, folding his arms. "We must honor the food you have prepared. And I must read the signs that are presented to me and accept that an anonymous author is, perhaps, meant to stay anonymous. It is God's will."

I can do nothing but head for the kitchen...to honor the food.

Main Course

*The guests share the main insights of
their mystical experiences.*

As I don the heatproof mitts and open the oven door to take out the fish, I wonder what Cloud might have revealed about himself if we hadn't been interrupted by the buzz of the timer.

"Probably nothing," a voice behind me answers, startling me enough that I almost drop the hot baking tray I'm in the process of lifting from the oven rack to the bench.

"Oh, sorry. Didn't mean to surprise you." And I recognize Francis's voice and ready laugh as I steady the tray by placing it on the firm surface. When I turn to face him, I can't help but smile at his apologetic look, and my smile broadens when I see that Pat is standing right next to him, tail wagging in obvious delight at his new friend and inclusion in the dinner party.

"I just thought I'd give you a hand carrying things to the table."

"Thanks, Francis. That would be great. Those dinner plates need to go in, and there's salad, and after I put this salmon and the barley risotto into serving dishes, they can go too. But before that, Francis, can I ask you how you knew what I was thinking when you came into the kitchen?"

"Did I know?" Francis is pulling an incredulous face, but I see the twinkle in his eyes. "Yes, okay, I knew. I could tell by your reluctance to leave the conversation, and then the distracted way in which you were opening the oven, that you were thinking of Cloud. And what you might have learned about his identity. But, the thing is, there must have been a reason that Cloud chose to write anonymously all those centuries ago. Maybe he will share that reason with us later; and perhaps that reason might be even more interesting than finding some superficial details about him."

I nod, realizing that there's wisdom in what Francis is saying, and he continues, "Look at Pat, here. He came to you without a name. You gave him a name and, by hearing it repeated over time, he learned to answer to that name. But the name is not the real essence of Pat, the dog. You know and love Pat because of. . . ."

"A rose by any other name would smell as sweet, as Shakespeare says. . . ."

"Ah, Shakespeare—a bit after my time, I'm afraid. But yes, I get the meaning, though in Pat's case, the smell of wet dog is not as readily appealing as the scent of a rose. Though, actually, I'd choose Pat any day over a flower. Wouldn't you?"

Pat seems to know exactly what Francis is saying about him, leaning into the side of Francis's leg with his full Labrador weight. And after Francis and I have organized dinner plates and dishes of food onto trays and head toward the dining table, Pat trots along beside us as if the dinner could not continue without him. He does, however, have the canine courtesy to acknowledge my stern eye on him as we enter the room by responding with a swift slink back under

Francis's chair in case I change my mind and eject him. I know Pat is fond of his warm bed in the corner of the kitchen, but there is no question that this evening he prefers the cozy company of the dining room.

"Da dah!" Francis announces with a flourish as he transfers the serving dishes onto the table while I distribute the dinner plates.

"What marvelous sustenance you are providing us with, Annie," enthuses Cloud. "Let us take a moment to feast our eyes on its beauty before we indulge our senses of taste and smell in the eating of it."

I am surprised by Cloud's suggestion, but it seems that my guests are comfortable with the idea and a quiet minute follows as they look from one dish to another, the gaze of some lingering a little longer here, others there.

"There is such a variety of colors and textures here," says Hildegard. "Please tell us about what you have prepared."

Suddenly, I feel quite shy but, knowing their interest is sincere, I reply, "It's a simple meal, really. Baked salmon fillets, barley risotto with spinach and mushrooms, and a green salad with figs and toasted sesame seeds. Also, in the pouring jugs, there's some lemon-butter sauce for the fish and a honey and balsamic vinegar for the salad. That's it! Now please, help yourselves and enjoy."

"Let me serve you first, Annie," says Francis, filling a plate with a selection from each dish and placing it in front of me before joining the other guests as they help themselves and each other. Drinks are replenished, too, and soon they are eating with obvious appreciation.

Cloud, seated to my right, puts his knife and fork down and, though inclining his head in my direction, clearly intends to include everyone when he says, "I noticed, Annie, that you seemed a little reticent to acknowledge the magnificence of this meal. It has taken time and effort and love to organize this. You can be pleased with yourself."

Before I can even begin to think of a response, Francis helps me out with, "Perhaps Annie is caught between honesty and humility."

Cloud claps his hands. "A good observation, Francis. But, really, humility and honesty go hand in hand. Because humility is nothing more than the true knowledge of ourselves as we really are. And really knowing ourselves has two components. The first is a true recognition of our gifts as well as our faults, failings, and weaknesses; it involves admitting that we are far from perfect—and this is the case for every human being. The second is realizing the great love that God has for us despite our lowliness. And, as it happens, knowing ourselves as we really are and coming to a full realization of God's unending love are so closely aligned that achieving the first is also achieving the second, and vice versa."

"It sounds so simple, so sensible, when you describe it in that way. To be honest, until now, I haven't had a very clear idea of what humility is. We don't talk about it today, really. In fact, from my observation, humility is misunderstood. It seems to be regarded as something negative, certainly not a sought-after quality, not at all popular in today's society where the instilling and building of self-esteem in each individual is perceived as the basis for happiness and success," I say.

"Ah yes, the self-esteem issue." Hildegard is nodding. "It can be a trap. I mean, of course, we all want to feel good, positive, about ourselves. That is as it should be. Each one of us—that is, the essence of our being—is made in God's image, so we are wonderful. But that's the point. We are made, created. God is the uncreated Creator."

"Of course, there is nothing wrong with nurturing a self-esteem built on the surety that we are made in God's image and are infinitely loved by God," reflects Margery, "but the problem for many today, as I see it, is that self-esteem is regarded as being related to one's achievements, one's possessions, one's looks and talents, and when any or all of these external things fail, self-esteem fails with it. In my case, I found self-esteem only when I faced the truth of myself and came to self-knowledge. Before that, I was operating out of false humility, wanting others to see me as humble by seeking their contempt and humiliation. And that, of course, was pride, the very antithesis of humility."

Hildegard raises her glass and tilts it in Margery's direction. "Congratulations on your insight and honesty, Margery. You were, perhaps, more honest about this than I was. And I think it's time I faced this particular failing of mine." Hildegard takes a good sip of her wine and then puts the glass down and places her interlocked hands on the table. She looks pensive as she begins, "You will recall that we talked earlier of some of the restrictions that were placed on women in medieval society. One of the most difficult to deal with, from my point of view, was negotiating the prohibition, imposed by the Church, whereby women were forbidden to preach. Now, I know that this prohibition originated with Saint Paul. Rather than give my opinion on whether the ban was based on accurate or inaccurate understandings of his words, I say only that as God created both men and women, and as all humans are equal in the eyes of God, and as God does all things, and all things well, then God's apportioning of wisdom and spiritual gifts are at the behest of God alone. That said, the Rhineland of the twelfth century was as it was, and men held authority in every sphere of endeavor. The Church was no exception, and so when God blessed and inspired me with great visions of the Divine glory, and when God opened my mind to greater understanding of prophesy and scripture, I knew that it was incumbent upon me to share those insights for the benefit of all. And, even though I obtained papal approval to disseminate those insights, the prohibition against women's preaching still pertained. The only option available to me, therefore—or so I believed—was the adoption of what is often now called a 'humility topos.'[1] That is, I assumed a persona of humility in my writings about God—I did not have to do so in my other works such as those on nature and medicine, nor in my music—relinquishing all authority over my work and positioning myself as God's messenger; the Church's male hierarchy would not prevail against God's choice of a spokesperson, even if it were a woman. This is not to say that I did not feel humbled by the gifts and insights God bestowed upon me, but more that I felt disappointed that I was restricted from proclaiming God's goodness more freely and widely. The humility topos in my theological works took the form of an allegory in which I told of a mighty king who took up a feather and commanded it to fly. Now, borne up by the air, the feather flew and, similarly, I was enabled to fly because I was borne aloft by God's command. And thus, I came to describe myself as a feather on the breath of God."

Cloud's tone is reassuring as he says, "A feather on the breath of God is a beautiful and very apt metaphor, Hilde-

---

1. A *topos* is a term used in literature to refer to a traditional theme or subject. In medieval times it was usually necessary for women to feign humility as they were not allowed to preach or put forward their own ideas in writing without the approval of the Church or other recognized male authority.

gard. And, if I may say, in my opinion, it was not false humility. It was a statement of true humility because you have acknowledged that you understood that you could accomplish nothing on your own and that any achievements and teachings you received were wrought in you by the grace of God to share for the help of others. And, in truth, male or female, all of us are God's instruments in our writings."

Hildegard and others around the table look to be mulling over these words, and I am thinking that Cloud's words make sense. What else was Hildegard to do in that time and situation?

It seems that Hildegard is entertaining the same conclusion. "You are wise, Cloud. Perhaps, then, it was a failure of courage, more than of humility. I took the line of least resistance for the sake of expediency."

"I don't see it that way," says Francis. "Your motivation was only the desire to share God's words and works, and that is courageous in itself."

"And, if I might add my support of you, Hildegard," says Julian. "I see no fault in what you did. But, if anyone is to confess to false humility, it is I who wrote of myself that I was a weak and frail and unlearned woman when, in truth, I had received a reasonable level of learning for a woman of that time." Julian's voice cracks a little.

Hildegard seems agitated. "Ah, that may be so, Julian, but remember that the measure of adequate learning in medieval times was one's proficiency in Latin, which was the written and spoken language of clerics and scholars who, by definition then, were only males. You wrote in your vernacular language, and by doing so you enabled so many more people to access your insights. Yes, I wrote in Latin, as was expected of me, as I was under the auspices of the twelfth-century Church, but it was not especially elegant Latin. In addition, as was the practice then, the 'learned' epithet was applied only to those who had access to education in the seven liberal arts—the trivium and the quadrivium—which, again, was exclusively limited to males.[2] So, if you are willing to excuse my inclusion of the humility topos, you must excuse your own."

"Precisely," agrees Richard. "You might call it 'expedience,' Hildegard, but in my opinion, you were both doing God's will in the way you worked within the limits of the age."

"And there is much to be said for expediency," opines Cloud. "As I have stressed to my students and readers of my texts: time is made by God for humans to use. We are temporal creatures. We live in time, but God is eternal. So, at the end of our days, we will be asked to give an account of how we used our time."

Richard straightens up in his chair, obviously very interested in this new turn the conversation is taking. "This is an issue of great importance, Cloud. I, too, have been at pains to draw it to the attention of those whom I was charged with counseling spiritually. In a short text that I wrote for an anchoress,[3] who had requested a guide on how to best serve

---

2. In the medieval period, the "seven liberal arts" were considered essential for the development of the thinking skills that marked a well-educated person. A student (male cleric) first worked through the trivium—grammar, logic, and rhetoric—and then moved on to the quadrivium—arithmetic, geometry, music, and astronomy.

3. The anchoress was Margaret Kirkby, enclosed at Ravensworth, North Yorkshire. Rolle wrote a number of texts for her, but the particular guide to which Richard is referring here is *The Form of Living*. See Richard Rolle, *Prose and Verse*, ed. S. J. Ogilvie-Thomson (London: Oxford University Press, 1988), 3–25.

God daily in her enclosed life, I reminded her that the duration of our lives is so short—barely a pinpoint—that we hardly exist at all. The other thing to keep in mind is that we do not know when our brief life will end, so it's vital that we make the most of whatever time we have. Therefore, it is prudent to be very cautious about choosing passing pleasures over the things that benefit us eternally."

"Quite so!" adds Cloud. "And if you think carefully about it, you will realize that time is so precious that God has given it to us in the form of one moment after another, always moving forward. We cannot go back. In any one of those moments, depending on the choices we make, heaven can be won or lost. In my era, we thought that the smallest unit of time was what was known as an *athomus*,[4] a measure so tiny that there are six of them in one second. That's almost the equivalent of what we might regard as instantaneous. Wonderful, isn't it?" Cloud is smiling at sharing these details and notices that I can't disguise my enthusiasm for this information, either. "What do you find most interesting about this, Annie?" he asks me.

"I'm fascinated by anything to do with physics," I confess. "And, as I listened to you, I was trying to imagine what a sixth of a second is really like. And then I was thinking that, now, we can measure units of time that are vastly shorter than an athomus. Not even to mention the unimaginable smallness of the quarks—and perhaps there is something even smaller—that constitute matter. And then I was thinking that, as you pointed out, in every tiny moment there are

---

4. Current estimates of the medieval opinion on the size of an athomus in relation to time is that there were about 20,000 of them in an hour; therefore each athomus was equal to one-sixth of a second.

countless possibilities and choices we can make. One moment, one choice. It's exciting, but it comes with a huge responsibility, and it's a timely—excuse the pun—reminder to be aware of that responsibility."

As I finish speaking, Francis gets up and walks behind my chair, briefly but firmly patting me on the shoulder as he moves on to stand behind Cloud's chair and pat his shoulder too. He looks between me and Cloud, saying, "You are a deep thinker, Annie. As for you, Cloud, I can barely keep up with you and your profound ideas but I know you have much to teach us."

"As do you, Francis," says Cloud, turning to look over his shoulder at Francis. "Your love of God is the perfect example of the melding of action and contemplation. Your path is one that follows Jesus unswervingly."

Francis steps away from Cloud's chair but remains standing behind it, his arms outstretched a little, and with a sparkle in his eyes. It strikes me then that even in his casual dress and easy manner, there is a power, an authority. I can picture him preaching in any situation and, without effort, winning people to God's love.

I realize that Margery must have been thinking something similar when she says, "Francis, please don't take this the wrong way, but you're a very attractive man."

I notice Hildegard tilt her head to one side and narrow her eyes as she asks, "Margery, I don't disagree with you, but I'm interested to know why you've been moved to make this observation about Francis?"

"Oh, Hildegard," sighs Margery, "it's a weakness of mine, I must confess. In my day, I had quite an eye for the men. We all have our failings, don't we? Of all the seven deadly sins, I'll admit that lust was at the top of my list."

"I admit a similar failing," says Richard, "though in my case, I disguised such feelings by condemning women. As the words in my text *The Fire of Love* will testify, I was often guilty of judging, even rebuking, women for dressing too richly, for adorning themselves in the latest fashion. Later, I came to see that these rebukes said more about me than them. In honesty, I think I took too much interest in the beauty of women, and I would have preferred that they made my life easier by not drawing my attention to them so often. Over the years, I saw myself as I really was and, toward the end of my life, was able to see women as equals and to admire their devotion to God and their holy calling."

Hildegard roars with laughter. "Such honesty from you both. I would like to hear more about this, but I think we'd be straying very far from our topic, don't you?"

I see Margery and Richard nodding in agreement. Francis, still standing behind Cloud's chair, has an amused look on his face.

Cloud, too, is smiling, and deftly gets us back on track by suggesting, "Perhaps Margery means that you have *charisma*, Francis."

"I'm not familiar with that word. What does it mean?" Margery asks.

"Well, we use it today to refer to people whose attractiveness or charm draws others to them and, in some cases, inspires others to follow them," I offer.

"Then Francis definitely has charisma," states Margery adamantly.

At this, Francis grins at Margery. "I don't mind a compliment or two now and then," he says, "but I'm certain that people followed me all those years ago because I was doing God's work."

"There is no doubt about that, Francis," agrees Cloud, "but it's an observed fact that those who devote themselves to God's work, especially to contemplative prayer, often become more attractive to others in their outward appearance, in line with the increasing inner beauty of their souls."

"Looking better is what we'd now call a 'fringe benefit' of the spiritual work," I add.

"Another term from today might also help explain this increased appeal, I think," says Cloud, "That is, when you're really working on your spiritual self, on your soul, the ego falls away, along with any false perceptions of yourself, and your true self is revealed. And as your true self is that part of you which is the image of God, then others see God in you; and what could be more appealing than that?"

"Well, that makes sense to me," agrees Francis. "If that's how God works, then that's how God works. As you said, Cloud, we're all God's instruments in whatever way we are called to share the message. I found my calling in walking in the steps of Jesus, embracing the gospels and, of course, Lady Poverty. Simplicity, humility, and love were the companions I desired, in company with the poor and the sick. And, as we've been speaking of choices, it was Jesus's Sermon on the Mount, the Beatitudes, in particular, that guided me. How beautifully Jesus nourished our hearts and minds by taking the things that we value on earth and turning them upside down. It is not the materially wealthy but the poor in spirit who will have the real kingdom, that of heaven."

There's unanimous agreement with Francis's words as he returns to his seat and, detecting a momentary lull in the conversation, I take my chance to comment to the group in general, "On that subject of sharing the message, you must notice many differences between your own times and our present day."

"The means of communication are definitely better; superficially at least," offers Hildegard. "When I received my visions, for example, I would have been very grateful for a voice-activated writing system such as today's iPhone and laptops have. Instead, I had to use wax tablets and a stylus."

"I didn't know that, Hildegard," says Margery. "Can you give us more details?"

I can tell Hildegard is warming to the topic as she dabs at her mouth with her napkin and then places it aside. "Well, I received my visions so immediately that I had to have an efficient method of recording them. For that reason, I had several tablets at hand, each one a flat rectangular piece of wood with a wooden border and covered in a layer of wax. Using a stylus—a writing implement with a pointed end and a spatula-shaped end for erasing—I could imprint my visions quickly into the wax as I received them and then pass the tablets onto my secretary, scribe, and faithful confessor, Volmar, for transcription to parchment."

"Handy as those tablets sound, Hildegard, the volume of your work is so extraordinary that the task must have been onerous, I imagine, especially with your duties as abbess and other demands on your time." I shake my head in a mix of admiration and incredulity. "I mean...excuse me...I hope you don't mind, but I need my memory prompts here," I stammer, hurrying to retrieve a small bundle of papers from the dining room cabinet's drawer. I rush back to the table and unfold them, aware that all eyes on me. "Um, a bit embarrassing, but I find all of your accomplishments quite overwhelming and so I've made a list of them. Actually, I have made a list on each of you. Notes on your works and writings are jotted all over these crumpled little pages." I feel my face reddening, and cast my eyes down as I add, "I hope you don't mind."

Hildegard slams her hands on the table so loudly I'm almost frightened to look up; but I do, and am relieved to see she is laughing. "Mind," she booms, "why would we mind? That's the whole point of us now. That's our service. That's how we can help. I know I speak for all when I say that those crumpled little lists of yours are jewels in my crown of posterity. Hopefully, that means that people are wanting to learn something of God's goodness through the reading of our works."

There are sounds of assent around the table.

"I agree so wholeheartedly with you, Hildegard, that I have decided to have a second helping of that delicious risotto," declares Richard, reaching for the dish. "As I was at pains to instruct those for whom I acted as spiritual advisor, it is never advisable to be overzealous in limiting one's food intake, because a healthy body is needed to support the spiritual life. Can I help anyone else?"

"Well, it is quite delicious. And, as I rely totally on the Lord's providence for my food, and as it is being provided so generously through our kind host, I'll have another helping please," says Francis, passing his plate to Richard.

Margery, suddenly coy, lifts her plate and says, "Perhaps I might indulge again, Richard, while you're offering."

"Oh, why not." And Cloud is in line for some more, too.

Serving spoon poised, Richard surveys the table. "What about you, Julian and Annie?"

"Thank you, Richard, but no, not for me," I respond.

"Nor me, thank you," says Julian. "But, while you're all enjoying the risotto, perhaps you'll tell us what's on your list, Annie."

I nod, and shuffle through my notes until I find the page on which I've copied notes about Hildegard's works. "Here it is. Permit me to read it to you as you eat. It's quite a long list." I pause a moment to scan my jottings and then proceed. "First, there's the work that I've most often heard about in relation to you, Hildegard, and that's *Scivias*, which, I believe means 'Know the Ways' (of the Lord), the first book of what's known as the *Visionary Trilogy*. The other two books—and from now on, I'm dispensing with the Latin titles because I definitely have no ability in that area—are *The Book of Life's Merits* and *The Book of the Divine Works*. Then there's...."

"Ah hmm," Hildegard interrupts with a cough and a wave of her hand. "Dear Annie, while I appreciate your diligence in assembling this list, I know that it's quite lengthy and, for the sake of your guests' continued enjoyment of this evening, may I suggest that you refrain from reciting its contents in detail lest we are all asleep by the time you complete it."

I'm not sure how to respond to this, and I'm thankful when Julian comes to my rescue with the suggestion that I summarize the contents by, perhaps, just naming the general areas and interests of Hildegard's many works. Others around the table seem happy with this compromise, too, and so I take a breath and oblige. "Okay. Well, in addition to the visionary trilogy, there are several works on natural science and medicine and a variety of miscellaneous works that include some biographies, discourses on the gospels, and explanations on the *Rule of Saint Benedict* and of symbols used in the writings of St. Athanasius. There are more than three hundred letters; there's even a secret language and cryptic writings as well as solutions to scholastic questions. There are more than seventy musical compositions, and even a play—a full-length musical drama. There's probably more, but that's my list."

Hildegard waves a dismissive hand again. "Oh, it sounds impressive in its quantity. And perhaps it is. As I've learned this evening, false modesty is to be avoided. So, if I may, I should like to simplify it for you." Hildegard does not wait for agreement and, instead, gets straight to the point. "Let us put aside the musical works and the play until later. They are lighter topics, best suited to be consumed with dessert. The biographies are really hagiographies—saints' lives—and I knew the stories well enough from oral sources, having heard them repeated often in my younger years. Most of the letters were of necessity for the business of running and maintaining and protecting the interests of our convent and the nuns for whom I was responsible; others were answers to requests for prayers or advice. The secret language and writings allowed me to communicate with my nuns confidentially, if required, and also provided distraction and training for the minds of my charges. The solutions to the thirty-eight questions were for sharpening my own brain in the area of philosophy. The works on natural science were part of my daily life and work—herbs for healing the ailments of my nuns and local people who came to our convent for assistance. Thus, as you'll see, there were many of my writings that were of practical everyday use, and not outcomes of the divine inspiration that prompted my visionary works and the elucidation of the scriptures. And it is of these latter that I would like to give more detail, if it pleases you."

This time, Hildegard waits for a response, and Richard obliges. "I know I speak for all when I say that we'd welcome details on your visionary works. However, I think we all agree that we would also enjoy a discussion on the lighter topics of your music and medical insights a little later in the evening."

"As you wish," Hildegard acknowledges and proceeds. "Permit me a short preface by way of describing something of the nature of my visions and then I will get to the heart of the topic. I had from my childhood experienced visions, sometimes accompanied by a voice, and usually in the form of flashes and swathes and interplays of light. Even as a child, I knew these were from God, and they continued throughout my time with Jutta and into my life as an abbess. But I did not speak of these occurrences until, at the age of almost forty-three, I received God's clear directive that I must write and share what I saw and heard. As previously, the visions of my middle life were received as a fiery light—I called it the Living Light—that engulfed my whole being. Often the blinding lights would be accompanied by clear, brightly colored architectural structures and images of mountains and animals and the beauty of the cosmos. I perceived these things not with my physical eyes and ears but with the eyes and ears of my soul. And with the visions and auditions came an infused ability to interpret them fully just as, suddenly and totally, the deeper meanings of scriptures were revealed to me. And not while I was sleeping or dreaming, but instead the visions would come to me as I was wide awake and still able, simultaneously, to observe what was happening in everyday life."

"You'd call that multi-tasking, wouldn't you, Annie!" grins Cloud.

"Ultra-multi-tasking," I reply with a smile.

"Apologies, Hildegard. Hope I didn't interrupt your flow of thoughts here," says Cloud. "It's just that I'm amazed to hear of all you've accomplished."

"No apology needed, Cloud. You know, I have to admit that, even though God's gifts to me were wonderful, there were times when I struggled to achieve all that was asked of me. For example, *Scivias* was a very difficult work to accomplish, in many, many ways. It took me over ten years to write and, when completed, it amounted to over one hundred and fifty thousand words.[5] I'm not surprised, then, that many readers today struggle to understand it. As you've requested to know something of this work, I shall try to honor that request, but I'm sure you will appreciate that a neat explanation of it eludes my powers."

"Key ideas. That's all we need." Margery speaks for all of us.

Hildegard nods. "For expediency's sake—as this is in our awareness this evening—I will concentrate on aspects that might pique your interest. However, please feel free to stop me if you're bored to sobs (as they say). So, *Scivias* is in three parts of varying length and, overall, attests to what I was divinely shown about the whole sweep of history and the scriptures—from the Creation to the Coming of Christ and the Redemption, through to ultimate salvation and the bliss of heaven—and the relationship of all these components to the way in which God's people should live their lives in order to gain heaven. Within this broad sweep, I was first shown detailed and exquisite images of such things as the Fall, the Choir of Angels, the structure of the universe, and the relationship of our bodies to our souls; in the second group of visions, I saw such wonders as the Trinity, Christ the

---

5. For a full-text translated edition of *Scivias* see Hildegard of Bingen, *Scivias*. Classics of Western Spirituality. Trans. Mother Columba Hart and Jane Bishop (New York: Paulist Press, 1990).

Redeemer, the Church and its sacraments, and Christ's Passion. Visions of salvation and the heavenly city were the main features of the third group. My method in explicating each vision was, first, to describe it in careful detail, then to consider the significance and meaning of those details, relating them to Holy Scripture and the teachings of holy Church."

"It was a vast undertaking," I say. "No wonder it took you more than ten years. I admit that I know little of the *Scivias*, but I do know that the visions included the 'cosmic egg.' Can you explain something of that?"

"Annie, you are an insightful soul," laughs Hildegard, "for if I describe and elaborate something of my cosmic egg vision it will serve as an example of my method in all the other visions (though, of course, one vision cannot tell the whole story). The cosmic egg represents the universe (as it was understood in the Middle Ages), full of symbolism in each of its components, because everything that is in creation under God has a meaning for us, and a connection back to its Creator. At that time, we saw everything—from the smallest flower to the farthest star—as composed of the elements of fire, water, earth, and air. And so, in this, my third vision, God showed me an immense shape, small at its top, full in its middle, and proportionally narrower at its bottom, just as an egg is shaped. And around the egg blazed fire, whirled by wind in parts, stirred by thunder and lightning. And inside, in various zones, were to be found watery air and soft rain, and a great, immovable earthy globe, and a mountain which was covered in darkness on one of its aspects, and bathed in great light on another. And the moon and stars shone. Now, this is a greatly abridged version of all that was to be seen in the egg but each element and fiery tempest and light and shade stand for aspects of omnipotent, incomprehensible

God. A globe of sparkling flames within the outer fire, for example, indicates the brilliance of the Son of God within, and as an outcome of, God the Father. The whirling winds are the all-consuming power of Almighty God, and the stars and moon have meaning, too, as the gospel tells us that 'There shall be signs in the sun, the moon, and the stars, and on the earth distress among nations confused by the roaring of the sea and the waves' (Luke 21:25). Some instruction to God's people follows about looking to saints and not to those who make idle predictions. There is much more to say, but I hope you have some idea of the scope and thrust of what God entrusted to me."

"Oh my goodness. Thank you, Hildegard, I now have an inkling of an idea of your enterprise," says Francis as he shakes his head. "I think we might need some more water or wine before we hear what else you have to say." And with that, he is stands up and goes around to each guest to top up their glasses as they require.

"I see that something is troubling you, Annie." Hildegard has her eyes fixed on me.

"I'll be honest, Hildegard. I'm having trouble grasping what you're saying. This will sound foolish, but when I think of an egg, I have to admit that I think of chickens and a barnyard, not the brilliance of the universe."

"Dear Annie, there is nothing wrong with that. God has made both the universe and the chicken, and in the egg of both there is abundant life. What is in the macrocosm of God's creation is also in the microcosm of everyday life. I am a woman of the twelfth century, and an abbess to boot! The world changes, only God does not change. My visions were grand and complex, and it was incumbent upon me to interpret them to the best of my theological and spiritual ability—

which, of course, God had bestowed on me. I saw my fiery visions in the context of my time and that served God's people then. But true prophecy and understanding does not end with the passing of the prophet. True prophecy reflects on the past, instructs the present in the manner in which the present has ears to hear and understand, and points to the future. For now, I will be satisfied if you take the cosmic egg and let it speak to you of God's goodness.

"That's very helpful. Thank you, Hildegard. I don't think I'll look at an egg in quite the same way ever again."

"In that case, my work is done. And, perhaps, if I now give the briefest overview of my two other visionary works, a little more insight might be gained."

Hildegard glances at me and the other guests and, receiving nods of agreement, she continues. "Of the *Book of Life's Merits*, I will say only that it's broadly about the links between the cosmos and our way to salvation but concentrates particularly on the vices and human weaknesses that separate us from God and the virtues that inform our repentance to lead us back to God. However, although informed by divine visions, I was inspired to present the subject matter in the form of dramatic dialogues between the vices and the virtues. Enough of that!

"And so to the third text of the trilogy, the *Book of Divine Works*.[6] This was the culmination of a lifetime of growing insights, visions, writings, prayer, and reflection. Here, under God's continuing guidance, many things came together for

_____

6. For a full-text translated edition, see: Hildegard of Bingen, *The Book of Divine Works*, trans. Nathaniel L. Campbell. Fathers of the Church Medieval Continuations (Washington: Catholic University of America Press, 2018).

me and I saw clearly that Christ's Incarnation both divided the Old and New Testaments and drew them together. Now, today—and I think this will interest you, Annie—I know that great physicists seek a 'Grand Unified Theory,' but I found mine in the Incarnation. It was the wonderful intrusion of eternity into history. The unfolding of history is the unfolding of time, but time will end. God will not end, nor will we, as we are in God."

Hildegard leans back in the chair and exhales loudly. She is tired, I know, from her efforts to condense a lifetime of visionary writing into a dinner-party conversation. The others seem to recognize the effort, too. I long to ask her about her famous idea of *viriditas*, when suddenly I realize that I have been staring at her, and she has noticed.

"Is there something else, Annie?" she asks, without a hint of impatience in her voice.

"*Viriditas*," I murmur.

"Ah, very well," she says, sitting forward again. "That is easily explained. *Viriditas* is greening; it is the life and growth principle of the spirit as well as of nature. We have our being in God; God is our true life, and it is God who creates and sustains life in everything—not just in humans but also plants, animals, and even gems. Creation is alive with verdant possibilities, pulsating with the hope and promise of renewal. Greening is woven through all my works—in my words and my actions—for God is always there."

All becomes quiet as, it seems, we each take a moment to reflect on creation and our place in the scheme of things. I see Julian shift in her chair as she reaches into the pocket of her dress to bring out something around which the fingers of her right hand are curled in a fist. With a movement that draws everyone's eyes to her, Julian raises the right arm with its clenched fist and then brings the forearm to rest on the table, the fist now upturned. Slowly she uncurls her fingers and there, lying on her palm, is what looks like a little ball. I lean in closer, as do my guests, and I realize that it is not a ball but a smooth, brown hazelnut.

"The first revelation of divine love which I received was, in part, about creation and our place in it," begins Julian. "This showing—the word I often use because in the English of the fourteenth century, *shewing* was the usual word for a vision or revelation—began, as I said earlier, with the living Christ on his cross. I saw his blood flowing from under the crown of thorns and, to my understanding, this crown encircled and contained everything that was to follow. For I understood that where I would be shown Jesus, I was also being shown the Trinity—Father, Son, and Holy Spirit—with Jesus in his Incarnation being the union between God and our souls."

Julian takes the hazelnut from her palm with the thumb and index finger of her other hand and holds it up for a few seconds so that we can see it more clearly. Then she puts it back on her palm and explains, "While I was seeing the actual physical sight of Jesus's blood flowing from under the thorns, God also showed me a spiritual sight of something lying on the palm of my hand. It was tiny, no bigger than this hazelnut. But it was not a nut. In fact, I could not think what it might be until God answered me by saying 'It is all that is made.'[7] And I was amazed because I realized I was being shown the whole of creation from God's perspective.

---

7. Julian of Norwich, *Showings* (Short Text), ed. Edmund Colledge and James Walsh. Classics of Western Spirituality Series (New York: Paulist Press, 1978), 130.

And, from there, creation is so small as to be almost insignificant. And I wondered how and why it survived at all. And again, I was answered that it 'lasts and always will because God loves it.'"[8]

"That is a wonderful vision of humility, of our smallness and yet our importance to God." Francis, who is sitting to Julian's right, reaches over and gently takes the hazelnut from her hand and puts it in his own. "How marvelous. What else was revealed to you, Julian?"

"In all, I received sixteen revelations, each one in three modes: *bodily*, by which I mean as we see things in the material world; *spiritually*, meaning not tangible but no less real and perceivable in a nonphysical way—*goostli* is the medieval English for it; and third, by *words* of clear explanation formed in my understanding. Some of the showings were short and straightforward in their meaning; others were of great length and complexity, but all highlighted God's love for us. And, knowing how much God loves us brought me to question the reason for suffering and sin in the world."

"Oh, big questions, Julian. Did you get an answer?" I am intrigued to know.

"Yes, although it took me a very long time—some years after the initial revelations—to come to a full understanding of the operation of sin in our world. First, I was shown—as was Hildegard in her visions—that God is in all things. And I was shown that God had made everything, and loves everything that is made. Furthermore, I was shown that all things are well done by God and that nothing is by chance. I dared to wonder, 'What about sin?' because I had not been shown

_____

8. Julian of Norwich, *Showings* (Short Text), 130.

sin. It came to my understanding that sin is nothing, but I did not understand how this could be, so my wondering persisted. And again, in my understanding, it was explained that God does everything, and everything that God does is good. Nothing God does is evil. Therefore, evil and sin are nothing. In fact, I saw that sin has no substance and is apparent only in the pain and suffering that it causes. Furthermore, I saw that humans make judgments, but the operation of God is through mercy and grace. Through God's grace, I was to receive more insight into the reasons for sin and suffering as my showings progressed. At one point, for example, I was shown that, while in the divine scheme of things evil is permitted, it is only permitted to a point and then thwarted by others' reactions to it so that good comes of it. Therefore, evil does not thrive unchecked."[9]

"But holy Church teaches that sin is real," says Cloud. "I can agree that God is all good, but I wonder, then, as you say, if sin results in pain and suffering for others, where does justice come in?"

"Cloud, you are voicing the very dilemma that I was experiencing," confesses Julian. "I wanted to be true to holy Church and its teachings but, as I've said, in all the things I was shown, I was not shown sin. And so, as my revelations proceeded, the issue that I had tried to push to the back of

---

9. The words here are the author's summary (with some elaboration) of Julian's insights into sin and the operation of evil in the world which she received in her Third and Fifth revelations. Similarities between St. Augustine's and Boethius's arguments on the subject of evil and Julian's insights have been noted by several scholars. See, for example: Denise Nowakowski Baker, *Julian of Norwich's* Showings: *From Vision to Book* (Princeton, NJ: Princeton University Press, 2014).

my mind came to the fore again for, like you, I had thought that if sin were not present in our lives then all would have been well. And God, with patience and love, gave me an amazing assurance wherein it was explained that sin is necessary because, although it has no substance itself and, as I knew, is recognizable only by the pain that it causes, that pain is passing and it has a purpose; while it is present, it leads to self-knowledge and the seeking of forgiveness. In this way, our Lord could assure me, and everyone, that all shall be well, right down to the smallest thing imaginable. We are called to trust in God because mercy and compassion will be given to us. I was cheered by this insight, but still I could not see how mercy could be shown to those whose sins are grievous."

"Yes, it's very hard for us to understand this, as we all know the pain that grave sin inflicts on others," reflects Margery.

"Very hard to fathom," agrees Julian. "And yet, my confusion was addressed in two ways. First, it was brought to my attention that human reason is so limited, so narrow in comparison to God's infinite wisdom, that we cannot possibly understand the mind of God. That is, only certain understandings and knowledge are open to us in our human condition. Second, certain understandings are hidden from us—'additional to needs,' as you might say now—but I was assured that, at the end of time—both regarding our individual lifetimes and in respect to all of us—God will perform a great deed which will make everything right. Now, what the exact nature of this great deed will be is in that part of understanding that is hidden from us; but in the part that is accessible to us through prayer and revelation, there is hope. God wants us to be happy, joyful, and full of hope because 'all shall be well, and all shall be well, and all manner of things shall be well.'[10] Now, Cloud, to your question about justice: I was shown that there are two types of judgment. The first is higher, because it belongs only to God; the second is lower, but still rightly operates in life—both in the Church and in civil law. And it is right that earthly justice is applied to those whose wrongdoing causes terrible pain and suffering to others and to themselves. How we reconcile the two justices is through prayer and trust in God's mercy. And, of course, always keeping in view the salvation that is ours through the death and resurrection of Jesus Christ."

"This really is a hopeful message, Julian. It must have put your questions to rest," I say.

"You would think so, wouldn't you, Annie? And yet, God went on to show me more about the issue in a wonderful allegory. But I think I will leave the description of this for later in the evening. For the moment, however, and on the same hopeful theme, I was also shown that we are right to approach God in prayer, in thanksgiving, and in beseeching. All are pleasing to God, and I was shown that, if our prayers are rightful and we approach in confident trust, God will always answer those prayers."

Margery is on her feet again, nodding and smiling at Julian's words, and moving around the table topping up the glasses as needed. She pauses next to Julian. "I'm very grateful for your words this evening, Julian. And, if it wouldn't tax you, I'd like to hear about your experience of God as our mother. People spoke of it at the time of my visit to you in Norwich, and I've often thought about it, being the mother of so many children myself."

---

10. Julian of Norwich, *Showings* (Long Text), 225.

"I'm happy to speak of it, Margery, but I want to remind everyone that the concept did not originate with me. In fact, it is recorded as first being elaborated by Clement of Alexandria in the second century. He used the image to refer to Christ feeding us spiritually in the Eucharist as a mother feeds her baby at her breast. Closer to my own time, St. Anselm took up the image and referred to God as our mother.

"As did a number of twelfth-century Cistercian monks, including my acquaintance, Bernard of Clairvaux,"[11] adds Hildegard.

"Exactly," confirms Julian. "And there were others. But, as you've asked, Margery, my experience of it in my showings was that God is our mother in that we are continually cared for, and nourished, and loved. But, note, I was also shown that God is our father, and our brother, and our spouse. God is beyond gender classification, as God is eternal and uncreated. Thus, God encompasses all aspects of the loving relationships that we experience in life and yet is beyond them, completely."

"Julian, there is so much to think about in what you've told us of your revelations." Francis has his elbows on the table, arms bent to allow his chin to rest in his hands. "But I know there is something more you have to tell, something that is the foundation and zenith of all that you saw."

"You are correct, Francis. So much was revealed to me that I spent a lifetime reflecting on it, and there is not time tonight to do any more than touch the surface. But really, one thing was above and below and through everything I was

---

11. Bernard of Clairvaux, an influential Cistercian monk and scholar, was instrumental in bringing Hildegard's visions to the attention of Pope Eugenius. Bernard and Hildegard corresponded by letter, but there is no evidence that they ever met in person.

shown. And that was love. Most poignantly, at the very center of the experience in the eighth and ninth revelations, I was, myself, close to death. At that point, as if in parallel to my own suffering, I was seeing the final torment of Christ on the cross: the drying and thirsting of his body. And I knew, when Christ uttered, 'I thirst,' that he was expressing a spiritual as well as a physical need, a longing for us, as well as for water. And I saw that of all the pains that we suffer, the greatest is to see the one we most love suffering. Thus, as I looked across the small space at my beloved Jesus on the cross, I forgot my pain and saw only his. And as he looked across at me, he was in the greatest pain because of my pain, and because of the pain that all humanity suffers in life. And I understood that we are on the cross with Jesus in our human pains each day. And I understood further, most clearly, that suffering and love are inextricably linked: the greater the love; the greater the pain. Mary, in her motherhood, suffered the greatest pain of seeing her son dying, and Jesus suffered the greatest pain in seeing his beloved mother, and all of us, suffer at his pain. We can all understand this. What parent does not suffer terribly when their child is suffering? If it were possible, we would choose to suffer in the place of the ones we most love because it is, actually, the lesser of two pains. And as I came to understand this, Christ suddenly changed his expression from one of pain to one of joy and, at this, I also came back from the brink of death. In this way, Christ showed me that, whatever our suffering in this life, we will be taken from woe into bliss in an instant. And I will share with you one last thing on this topic, and it is something that was given to my understanding long after my revelations. Over the years, I had asked God many times, and most fervently, what the deepest meaning of my showings was. And, finally, in prayer, I was answered that the meaning was love. And I asked who showed me all this, and I was answered, 'Love.' And I asked why I was shown it, and I was answered 'for love.' I need say no more."

Those at the table are quiet once more. I know that, like me, they are reflecting on Julian's words. Soon, though, my mind switches to my role as tonight's host and I'm wondering how to proceed from here. Would I break the mood if I clear the dishes from the table? I smile inwardly at my everyday musings in the face of such spiritual wisdom and beauty. I am deciding that I have to look on my current thoughts as valuable feedback on the subject of self-knowledge when Richard breaks the silence.

"Your revelations are profound, Julian, and yet, as you say, they all come down to one thing: love. I, too, was shown that God is love and, thus, that love is the center of all our yearnings. I have to say, however—and this is said in real, not false, humility—that my mystical experiences and apprehensions of love are much more . . . I'm trying to think of the right word here . . . well, more focused on sensual and sensory experience, but real indicators of God's love, nonetheless."

"The love of God can be revealed in countless ways, Richard," Hildegard assures him. "Please, tell us something of your experience."

"Very well, I shall do my best, in the interests of variety," he grins. "As I told you earlier this evening, my entry into the solitary life was rather dramatic. I had become very unsettled during my time studying theology. I realized that I didn't want to study *about* God; I wanted to experience God. That was my heartfelt intention. And, acknowledging that, I changed my life accordingly. For almost three years, living largely in solitude, I devoted myself to prayer. At that time, God blessed me with an extraordinary gift: I felt what I could describe only inaccurately, and only metaphorically, as 'the fire of love.' The surprise was that, despite my certainty of its spiritual origin, it was a real sensation, a bodily sensation, an actual heat around my heart, a warmth that fired my whole self with love of God and, since its first occurrence, has not left me. Often I've written about it using the Latin word for warmth, *calor*, but no word is truly adequate. And all the more so because it brought with it other sensations. There was an amazing sweetness for which I've used the word *dulcor*; this was another physically perceived sensation that encompassed all my soul. It was not as we might think of sweetness today. Now, sugar is the product we most likely associate with sweetness but, during my lifetime in the fourteenth century, sugar was a rare commodity. Medieval sweetness for food and drink was usually obtained from honey and, in many ways, the rich viscosity of honey and its production by the living, working ingenuity of bees, makes it a better symbol of the sweetness I experienced. But it is still a weak reflection of the real thing. And, as I mentioned earlier, there was also *canor*—song, melody, harmony—that engulfed my soul and turned all my feelings toward heavenly praise. Thus, my sense of touch was engulfed by warmth, my senses of taste and smell were enveloped in sweetness, my hearing was filled with exquisite melody, and all sensation coalesced into an all-consuming feeling of joy and love of God that concentrated on the eye of my heart so that God was ever in my sight."

Richard stops speaking and stares for some seconds into the dancing flame of one of the table's candles. Then he takes up his glass and has a serious sip of his wine.

"What a moving summary of the mystical gifts you have received, Richard," says Cloud. "How did they affect your subsequent devotion?"

"Well, of course they affirmed that my contemplation was pleasing to God, and they spurred me on in humility and self-knowledge by reinforcing the wonder and the mystery that is God. In addition, they drew my attention more acutely to the necessity of being aware, of being awake, to the workings of God in my soul. And with that awareness, I was more able to share God's love with others. For example, I wrote for one of the religious women under my spiritual direction a guide entitled *Ego Dormio*, being, as you would know, an abridged version of *ego dormio et cor meum vigilat, 'I sleep but my heart awakes'* (Song of Solomon 5:2). I frequently pray that everyone can feel the awakening of God's love in their hearts."

"I confess that I have had some similar experiences, but I am not the poet that Richard is," says Margery. "Still, sometimes I had such sweet odors assail my sense of smell that I thought I could forgo food and live on the fragrances instead. And sometimes my physical ears heard heavenly melodies that were so real that they blocked out the sound of someone speaking directly to me. And, at a later time, but no less powerfully, I too was blessed to receive the burning fire of love in my breast. These sensual apprehensions were a wonderful comfort to me, a confirmation that I was indeed on the true path to God, but it remained a difficult path nonetheless."

"That's understandable, Margery," says Julian. "As we've discussed, you were a lay woman, a wife and mother, without the official approval of the Church for your chosen life of prayer and pilgrimage. And, without Church support, your behavior and shows of sensual apprehensions would have been regarded with suspicion by many. However, with the

Lord's help you prevailed, and for that you are to be commended, not condemned."

"And yet, I cannot help but wonder what my gifts have contributed to others."

"Margery," I comment, "you wrote the first autobiography in English—a book prompted by your love of God. That is an example in itself. You were a brave woman who followed the path that God set you upon."

"Very difficult for you, Margery," Richard agrees. "But, as Annie has said, your experiences of God's love yielded a very important result."

"You are very kind. I suppose that some today do know of my book," Margery smiles at Richard before turning to Cloud to ask, "What about you, Cloud? Your book, *The Cloud of Unknowing*, is definitely a spiritual classic. You've shared some interesting points about humility and self-knowledge and time during our meal, but what of your own experiences? We'd all appreciate hearing about them, I'm sure."

Attention focuses on Cloud. He folds his arms, stares back at Margery with his lips pursed, and then smiles. I am taken by the way in which Cloud, and all my mystical guests, give their whole attention to whatever they are speaking about, and to whomever they are speaking. It is an approach that makes me feel valued in their company.

"Very well, dear friends," begins Cloud. "I shall say a little something about my own spiritual life. As we know, God calls each of us in different ways. Some are called to live a secular life of work and family, others to live the communal life of a monastery, others to the solitary life, and still others to a mixed life of prayer and action. I was called to a life of contemplation."

"Is contemplation the same as meditation?" I ask.

"It's a good question, Annie. Both are forms of prayer, but meditation, on the one hand, springs from our human desire to connect with the spiritual side of our being and usually involves the use of the imagination, or the emotions, or even a physical point of concentration such as the flame of a candle, to shift the focus from the physical to the spiritual. Contemplation, on the other hand, uses no intermediaries—no candles, no thoughts, no senses, no images—and is the work of God in the soul. That is why I said that I was called to the contemplative life, because, even though it might seem that I was seeking God and therefore found my way into contemplation, I only found the way because God was seeking and calling me, and I heard and responded. To honor that calling, it is necessary to work at putting aside things of the material world, including thoughts and feelings, and to aim instead for the higher things that are of God."

I'm aware that I'm thinking, wondering, doing the very thing that Cloud has learned to put aside when he is contemplating. I have to ask, "How do you manage to do this, Cloud?"

"With God's grace, of course, Annie," replies Cloud. "But, that doesn't make the contemplative life easy. We are called, but then it is our task to fulfill the call. Remember how we talked about the choices that we make in every consecutive moment? Well, contemplatives are also making the choice that, in all moments, they are directed toward God, and only God. Not wanting to promote myself here, but since Margery has already mentioned it, allow me to refer to my text, *The Cloud of Unknowing*. This I wrote for a young man of twenty-four, called to the contemplative life, who sought my guidance on how best to pursue it. Of course, I cannot 'teach' someone how to contemplate; it is God who leads and instructs. I can simply offer insights from my own experience. And my main insight is that 'God may well be loved, but not thought.'[12] That is, we can attain God only through love. There is nothing new or surprising in this. We have been talking at length about the primacy of love, about God as love. But, I suppose that my approach to love has its own features. So note that although my text has the word 'unknowing' in its title, I do not say that God cannot be known. Instead, I say that the means to truly knowing God is through love. Therefore, to truly know God, we must forget, put aside, what we have come to rely on in our lives and strive only for God. And to do this, I advised my young charge, and later readers, to put themselves in an in-between space in which they have a cloud of forgetting—of all worldly things and all material attachments—below them and a cloud of unknowing—of God—above them. And within that 'no-where' situation, they are to wait and think of nothing, and do nothing but long for God with the firm intention of piercing through that cloud of unknowing a sharp dart of love."

"But aren't you using images, and therefore the imagination, with those clouds of forgetting and unknowing? And don't you advise that images are not part of contemplation?" queries Margery.

"You are astute, Margery. But it's a fact of our human condition that we have to communicate, for the most part, with words. No words are adequate in our communication

---

12. *The Cloud of Unknowing and The Book of Privy Counselling*, ed. Phyllis Hodgson, EETS. o.s. 218 (London: Oxford University Press, 1944), 26.

about God. The clouds are indeed images, but I try to encourage my aspirants to 'be' between those two clouds rather than concentrating on them as a means of attaining God, if you see the difference." Cloud looks at Margery hopefully.

Margery doesn't look convinced, and I'm not feeling certain about this either, so I'm grateful when Richard tries to clarify, "I think you're advising that the aim is simply to be. To put oneself out of the way of all material attachment and thought, and simply to be aware of one's *being*—one's being in the presence of God."

"That's about as clear an explanation as I could hope for, Richard. Thank you," says Cloud. "To be honest, contemplation is simultaneously the simplest and the hardest work to do. It is the simplest because all that is needed is love, longing, and desire for God; and in the longing and the love, God is there; God is love. It is the hardest work because, in human life, there are so many conflicting drives and distractions that the intention to focus on God, and only God, seems almost impossible."

Suddenly, Francis gives a loud sigh and, a second later, Pat lets out a very similar sigh from his spot under Francis's chair. I watch as Francis bends down and gives Pat's fur a good ruffle; and then he straightens up, sighs a second time, scratches his head and then rubs the stubble on his chin before saying, "Oh, Cloud, you are speaking about the great mystery that is God. As you say, we cannot reach God by thinking about it. We can only love. Loving longing, holy desire—simplicity itself. Truth itself. That really resonates with me. And I understand your point about God being so far beyond our rational comprehension that all words and no words are equally inadequate in our attempts at describing the divine essence. And yet, for me, God is perfectly knowable in the Word made flesh."

"I would never disagree with you about that, Francis. It's just that, in my way, I was drawn to seek and find God with a method known as *via negativa*. That's an approach to the spiritual life, and the communication of it, that involves the stripping away of all material, mental, and emotional distractions, and all words and images and mediations that are so often used in drawing near to the love of God. Its origins lie deep in the early Church's expounding of what is called mystical theology.[13] Even the omitting of my name and details of myself from my writing were sincerely prompted by my wholehearted conviction that nothing should come between God and the soul. I was simply the messenger for my reader, not the initiator of the contemplation. My choice of this approach in no way means that I denigrate other approaches; it is just that this worked best for me. It enabled me to look at myself and to see myself as I truly was. I looked not in a physical mirror at my material self, but rather, I looked in the mirror of my soul where I saw a humble darkness, an absence of self that was full of God, because God is in me, in all of us, as the very cause of our being.[14] I speak of mirrors because they are fascinating things. In the Middle Ages, they were

---

13. Mystical theology is that branch of theology that is based on experiential rather than intellectual knowledge of God. Although it has its origin at least as early as Clement of Alexandria (c.150–215 AD), the Cloud author's main influence is Pseudo-Dionysius, a Syrian monk of the early fifth century, whose work on mystical theology and the *via negativa* was translated into (Middle) English by the Cloud author under the title, *Dionise Hid Divinite* ("Dionysius's Mystical Teaching").

14. For the Cloud author's discussion on the mirror see *The Book of Privy Counselling*, 136.

not of the same good clarity that they are today but, still, they enabled people to look at themselves. However, then as now—and as we discussed earlier about mistaken self-esteem —people tended to see only the good and poor aspects of their physical appearance, without a thought for their true selves, their interior selves. Many centuries before my life in the fourteenth century, the great St. Augustine stressed that God is the source of all reflection. And it is true that the human eye must have a light source in order to reflect a mirror image. God is my light source and my reflection. Without God, I am an absence."

"Oh, Cloud, that explains a few things about you," I say, as Francis winks in my direction, in our mutual recognition of his earlier words to me in the kitchen about Cloud's reasons for anonymity.

Julian takes everyone around the table into her benevolent glance. "I think we've all done well in sharing some of our deepest mystical insights. We know that, theologically, these are difficult things to comprehend. The Trinity, for example, makes no sense to the rational mind; but I was shown in my revelations that the Trinity is about a dynamism, a dynamic relationship between the Creator, the Word, and the Spirit, and in that is all we need; in that is all our longing. But it still remains a mystery to us. We just have to trust in God and proceed with love, and all shall be well."

"You're right, Julian," responds Francis. "The mystery of the Trinity, the immensity of God, the courtesy of God coming into our souls, the Incarnation, all these things and more are beyond our comprehension and bring us back to how humble we are compared to the brilliance of God."

"But how can we be certain we are on the right path?" asks Margery. "I mean, I see how confidently you have all proceeded in God's plan as it was revealed to you. But, speaking truthfully, I am still, after all these centuries, plagued by doubts."

"Doubt is part of the human condition," explains Cloud. "But you know Margery, I have no doubts about you and your love of God, nor any doubts about God's love of you. And perhaps this will help you: I know with certainty that 'it is not what we are, nor what we have been, but what we intend to be that God sees with his all-loving eyes.'[15] That is, we are weak and fallible in our human nature, but if our intention, our will, is directed to God, and in our deepest intention we long only to be aligned with God's will, then we are assured of reaching our longed-for destination. The desire is the attainment."

"That's such a hopeful message. Thank you, Cloud. Thank you all for your insights," I say, bringing my hands together in a prayer gesture and bowing my head to each of my guests in turn around the table.

"Thank you, Cloud, thank you everyone. How fortunate I am to be in such company," announces Margery, greatly moved by Cloud's final words. As I watch, however, Margery's expression changes and she looks confused, distracted. She starts to adjust the bangles on her arms. Suddenly, she springs up from her chair and rushes over to the full-length decorative mirror on the far wall of the dining room. Everyone is looking now as she positions herself directly in front of it, and starts to smooth the folds of her colorful dress over her ample hips. The candles on the sideboard to the left of the mirror wall flicker and bounce in response to the air in the room, and the flickering increases then di-

---

15. *The Cloud of Unknowing*, 132, (trans. Carmel Bendon).

minishes, increases, diminishes, highlighting different aspects of Margery's reflection as she gazes intently at herself and says, "I was fond of mirrors in my life. Vanity. I did want to change my life, but I did not have your insights, Julian, nor your strength of character, Hildegard. And I've sometimes wondered if. . . ."

Margery does not finish her thought. Instead, she is transfixed and I, in turn, am transfixed watching her as I feel time slow down, that one tiny athomus that Cloud was talking of seeming to stretch into a long vertical line as I sit glued to my chair and observe Margery falling, falling, falling . . . and finally landing on the floor on her back, her head missing the sharp corner of the base of the dining room cabinet by an inch at the most. I am frozen to the spot, the movement around me a blur. . . . I see Francis spring to his feet . . . see Hildegard run to Margery. I see that Margery is shaking; no, vibrating . . . violently; her body is jerking, her limbs are shuddering. And Cloud is rushing to her, and Richard is there too, while Julian is suddenly next to me, assuring me, "All shall be well." I see Margery stop vibrating; lying deathly still on the floor. And I am not assured, and nothing seems to be well.

Dessert

The mystics share some surprising and "lighter" insights into their lives and works.

Margery is still on the floor, but her limbs are at ease now and her eyes are open. Hildegard kneels and places her left hand on Margery's forehead. I notice Hildegard's right hand reaching into the pocket of her dress. She takes something out of it. I can't see what it is, but it's small enough to be enclosed by her fist. She whispers to Margery, and then I see Margery nod and open her mouth slightly. Hildegard places something in it. After a minute or so, Cloud and Francis are helping Margery to sit up. Richard has brought cushions from the living room to prop behind her so that she is comfortable. Julian stands nearby, a cup of wine in her hands at the ready for Margery. Pat pushes his way into the center of the tableau to lay his head on Margery's extended legs, and it is a relief to see her reach out her hand to stroke the dog.

"Should I call a doctor?" I ask, hovering nervously at the back of the "first responders."

"Whatever for?" asks Hildegard. "She has the best care available, right here. I am a very competent medical practitioner, and Francis is capable of performing healing miracles; Richard and

Cloud have enough faith and insight to guide us through anything; and everyone here is able to pray for Margery's return to health before the next part of our meal is served."

I'm not convinced, but I see color returning to Margery's face, and she is smiling at those around her. Then she places her hand over her mouth and removes something that she hands back to Hildegard before saying to me, "I'm perfectly well now, thank you. Don't trouble yourself, Annie. It was just one of my falling sickness episodes."

"Falling sickness? That sounds serious, Margery."

Margery replies, "Oh no, Annie. It happens to me regularly. And I always recover quickly. No need to fuss. Actually, if you, Francis, and Richard, can help me to my feet, I'll be ready to go on with the dinner."

"Well, if you are sure you're feeling better, might I suggest that we, at least, move our dinner to the living room," I say, looking from Margery to the other guests. "There we can get Margery comfortable on the sofa, extend her legs and put a warm rug over them. And then we can all take a seat around the fire and enjoy our dessert and look after Margery at the same time."

A chorus of "Good idea, excellent idea, Annie," sounds as I lead the way back to the living room and begin re-arranging the sofa cushions so that Margery can recline comfortably. As I've come to expect of my guests, nothing perturbs them. They have Margery in place in no time and are already shifting the seating around the coffee table so that we can all gather easily. I see Richard stoking the fire, too. While they're occupied, I hurry to the kitchen and, as I take the apple tart from the fridge, I'm feeling very glad that I had prepared it—up to its final stage—earlier in the day. Now all I have to do is make the apricot glaze for the top with its neatly arranged circles of soft, thin slices of apple. It doesn't take long to heat the jam and lemon juice together, and then I brush the glaze over the tart. I pop it in the oven to warm, and then it's back to the living room.

"Annie, don't rush," warns Margery as I propel myself into the room. "Perhaps you need a drink. You're very pale."

"No, Margery. As long as you are okay, then I am too," I reply but, as I take a seat, I'm grateful for the glass of water someone hands me. After a mouthful or two I feel able to ask, "Are you able to tell me about your falling sickness, Margery?"

"Of course, Annie. I have told you about my gift of tears and sometimes, while in the midst of those tears, or some other random phenomenon, something comes over me and I fall down, just as I did this evening. And after I have fallen, people have reported that I twist my body, first one way, then the other, and that my complexion takes on a strange pallor. During my lifetime in Bishop's Lynn and other places I visited, I was not the only person to fall down inexplicably and twist around. It was regarded as an affliction, and sometimes an evil one at that. The name 'falling sickness' was given to the occurrence, and people who suffered from it were often shunned or treated with suspicion."

"It sounds to me like you were having seizures of some sort, perhaps epilepsy. Well, that's what we would call it today. We know that it's the result of some kind of electrical activity in the brain and there's certainly no evil associated with it. Actually, as far as I know, there are now many effective treatments."

"It does my heart good to hear you speak of my illness in this way, Annie. I knew God, and not evil, was working in me, but still it was a heavy burden to bear."

"No, certainly not evil," I repeat. "In fact, it's possible that, in some cases, the opposite might be true. What I mean—and I'm definitely no expert—is that I've read about research into what is now termed 'neurotheology.' From my limited understanding, it's the study of links between the human brain and spirituality. On scanning the brains of people with temporal lobe epilepsy, for example, some researchers have found that the misfiring of certain normal neurons in these lobes—on either side of our head, near our ears—can increase the likelihood of spiritual visions and experiences. Now, this might at first seem to discount religious insights and, in fact, many scientists argue exactly that, but some neurophysiologists are not so sure and have even suggested that it's possible that the temporal lobes are the 'sites' of spirituality and that, in fact, the brain is in some way 'hard-wired' for God."

"That makes sense to me," says Richard. "I know very little about science, but I do know about my own experience; and perhaps God has designed these parts of the brain to which you refer, as some kind of receptors for greater awareness of the divine presence. Mind you, I've found that my heart does an excellent job of receiving the wonderful certainty of God's love."

"Well said, Richard," agrees Cloud. "What do you think, Hildegard?"

I notice Hildegard is frowning when she answers. "Those lights and flashes and colors in front of my eyes. I have had occasion to read a noted modern neurophysiologist's assessment of my visions. His diagnosis, as he called it, of not only the preceding lights but the visions themselves was that I was suffering from migraine with scintillating scotoma.[1] Now, I

---

1. Charles Singer, a British historian of medicine and science, was the first to attempt to make a diagnosis of "migraine" in regard to Hildegard. See Charles Singer, "The Scientific Views and Visions of Saint Hildegard," in *Studies in the History and Method of Science*, ed. C. Singer

do not say that he is incorrect. Perhaps I did suffer these headaches that he details; but it does not follow that my visions were any less real. He has his scientific paradigm in which to work; I have a divine paradigm. And I say that God works in mysterious ways and the opening of my understanding to the full and marvelous workings of the Divine may well have been wrought in me via a physiological affliction, as we have witnessed in the case of Margery. Many people excel in God's work after their bodies and minds are put to the test by suffering or illness or accident."

"Cause and effect, as they say. But we must not forget the 'first cause' of all causes and effects, and that is God," Cloud remarks.

"On that positive note, I think it's time I brought in our dessert," I announce as I stand to head to the kitchen, waving away offers of assistance with the task. As I take the tart from the oven, I'm relieved that it looks even better after being heated. The pastry edge is crisp and golden, the apples soft but the overlapping slices holding their shape perfectly. I transfer it very carefully to a serving plate and then onto the tray. I also take from the refrigerator the bowl of whipped cream that I had earlier enhanced with a hint of vanilla and cinnamon. With dessert bowls and spoons on the tray, along with a serving slide and some fresh napkins, I'm ready to return to the living room.

There are "oohs and ahs" as I place the tray on the coffee table. False modesty aside, I admit that it does look good. And soon I am slicing the tart, topping it with the cream, and

_____

(Oxford: Clarendon Press, 1917), 51–55. More recently, the neurologist Oliver Sachs took Singer's opinion further and reduced all aspects of Hildegard's visions to causation by migraine. See Oliver Sacks, *Migraine* (Berkeley, CA: University of California Press, 1993).

serving it to my guests who sit happily with napkins across their laps in readiness.

"Delicious, Annie," declares Richard after his first mouthful. "Where did you learn to bake this?"

"Thank you, Richard. I often make this for special guests. I didn't really learn to bake it from anyone in particular, but it's based on a recipe that a French friend shared with me many years ago when I visited Paris."

"I have always thought I'd like to visit Paris," muses Margery. "I have had the opportunity to travel to many places but never Paris."

"Where have you been, Margery? And why did you go to many places?" I ask. "Wasn't travel unusual in the Middle Ages, especially for women?"

Margery, in her semi-reclined position on the sofa, stretches toward the coffee table to put her bowl down carefully. There is still some tart left in it so I know she is warming to the subject, wanting to give all her attention to her reply. "I'll answer your 'why' question first. Two things spurred me to travel. First, as I've already shared, it was that I was often beset by doubt about the authenticity of my calling and this propelled me to places far and wide to seek validation from men in authority in the Church, and holy people—like you, Julian—to whom I could tell of my love of God and the experiences that I had received. Second, I longed to walk in the steps of my Savior and of saints everywhere, and to go on pilgrimages to receive all the graces attached to those holy journeys.

"As to the 'where,' my journeys of validation were centered in England, which, of course, was my home and, therefore, the place I most needed to be accepted as authentic. But there were places of holy pilgrimage in England, too, and these naturally drew me. So, on various occasions, my travels there took me to Leicester, York, Bridlington, Hull, Beverley, Lincoln, London, and Ely, to name just a few. And of course, as I've said, there was Norwich where I conferred with Richard of Caister and, most significantly, our dear Julian. At another time, I met with Thomas Arundel, the archbishop of Canterbury. Interspersed between my traversings of England were my undertakings of great and arduous pilgrimages to the holiest of places. In 1413, at the age of forty, I set out from my home and traveled to Venice to sail from there to the holy city of Jerusalem. On the return journey, I went from Venice to Assisi—where I prayed to you, Francis, in your chapel of the Porziuncola—and then to Rome, not returning home until after Easter 1415. Then, in 1417 and into the following year, I journeyed to Santiago de Compostela, sailing there and back from the port of Bristol. And, in 1433, prompted by the death of my dear son who had come to England to visit me with his Prussian wife—and somewhat reluctantly as I was growing old by this time and had always a fear of tempest at sea, even though God had assured me that I would not perish by drowning—I agreed to accompany my daughter-in-law back to her home in Danzig. As it happened, our ship was blown off course, onto the shore of Norway, and it was there that we stayed for the holy period of Easter. But God, whose word can never be doubted, ensured that we got back on course and arrived at our destination safely. I remained in Danzig for a few weeks, all the time wondering how I would return home, because I was terrified of returning by boat and, furthermore, I had no companions with whom to travel."

"You are courageous and adventurous, Margery. I am aware of the sort of dangers you must have faced along the way as we have some travels in common," says Francis, taking the spoon from his mouth and placing it gently back into the bowl on his lap. "Obviously, I've been to Assisi, and to Rome, of course, to obtain the papal approval for the order. During 1221 and 1222 I undertook a preaching tour through southern Italy. And before that, in 1219, eleven of my companions and I went to Egypt, only to be brought before the sultan when we crossed the Saracen lines. With God's grace, the sultan gave his permission for us to travel into the Holy Land and, by God's further grace, I managed to secure a continuing presence of our friars in the position of guardians of the most holy of places."

"And the Franciscans have a representation there, at the Church of the Holy Sepulchre, to this very day." I suddenly register that I have interrupted Francis, and quickly apologize.

"You didn't interrupt, Annie, no apology necessary," he says, already going back to eating his apple tart.

"Okay, thanks Francis. I'm just quite amazed at how far and wide both of you have traveled. Journeying must have been very difficult and fraught with dangers," I reflect, shaking my head at the very idea of it.

"It was dangerous, especially for a woman. But no one willingly traveled alone," explains Margery, her color now completely returned to normal. "During my lifetime, I knew of an author named Geoffrey Chaucer and . . ."

"Oh, now I have to interrupt." Julian sounds excited as she goes on, "I know of Chaucer. I had occasion to read his translation of *The Consolation of Philosophy* by Boethius."

"Proof again, Julian, that you are far from being 'unlearned,'" insists Hildegard.

"Well, as I've said, it was the English translation. But an excellent text, nonetheless. The Austin friary near my anchorhold had an impressive library, and I was permitted access to a number of its holdings.[2] I confess I also know a little of Chaucer's *The Canterbury Tales.*"[3]

"And that's just the book I was about to mention as, no doubt, you guessed," says Margery.

"Yes," nods Julian, "such a wonderful collection of tales."

"And the thing that is especially pertinent to our present discussion," continues Margery, "is that the medieval pilgrimage is the basis for this great work. For those of you who don't know, allow me to elaborate. Chaucer begins his tales by explaining that once spring settles over the land and the hardships and restrictions of winter are passed, people who were able to do so gathered to set out on a pilgrimage, which then meant a journey to a religiously significant destination in the hope of obtaining a spiritual benefit, whether that benefit was personal—as in securing the answer to a prayer or petition at the shrine of a holy person—or one that was bestowed by the Church—as in the case of the granting of indulgences, for example. Many pilgrimages were made by those unable to travel far; in these cases, people went to the

---

2. Scholarly research finds strong evidence that Julian was well acquainted with Boethius's text. In addition, for elaboration of the contention that Julian also had access to the library of the Austin friars in Conisford, Norwich, see Carmel Bendon Davis and Joseph C. Quy Lam, "'The Parable of the Lord and Servant' The Salvific Memory: Gracious Predestination in Augustine and Julian of Norwich," in *Louvain Studies* 34 (2009–2010): 312–35.

3. For edited Middle English versions of both *The Canterbury Tales* and *Boece* (Chaucer's translation of Boethius's *The Consolation of Philosophy*), see Geoffrey Chaucer, *The Riverside Chaucer.* ed. F.N. Robinson (Oxford: Oxford University Press, 1988, reprinted 2008).

shrines of local saints. But it was the aim of many pilgrims—and I was certainly one of them—to test the dedication of their love and commitment to God by undertaking the more arduous and lengthy journeys to the great pilgrim destinations of Rome, Compostela, and the holy city of Jerusalem. Pilgrimage routes crisscrossed continental Europe and the lands surrounding, and including, the Holy Land. In truth, there were economic advantages to be gained by those who set up inns and other services for pilgrims along these routes.

"And, lest you think I'm rambling and have moved far from my point about Chaucer, well, I'm coming to the connection. That is, even with the availability of some basic comforts, a pilgrimage was hard and the medieval roads were dangerous. Pilgrim inns were filthy and usually required guests to share a bed with two, or three, or even more, travelers. The food was frequently adulterated and the wine was always watered down. Outside the towns, along the way, desperate people—hungry or diseased, or both—lurked near the paths, ready to assail anyone who was foolish enough to travel unaccompanied. The fact, then, that Chaucer tells of the Canterbury pilgrims gathering at an appointed time at the Tabard Inn was representative of the usual practice of pilgrims organizing themselves to make their pilgrimage in the company of others. On my pilgrimages, I was never fortunate enough to have company as pleasant as Chaucer's group. Sometimes I had no company at all."

"This is why I think you were exceptionally brave, Margery," I say.

"Determined, dedicated, might be better words," Margery suggests. "But in all my travels, I had my dear Lord with me and, remember, I was a medieval woman. Dangers and hardships were expected by pilgrims then because, as everything in the medieval world was understood to be full of meaning, a pilgrimage was seen as the living equivalent of our overall spiritual journey from birth to death. Throughout life we meet disappointments, heartbreaks, ill health, unexpected losses and sometimes gains, good and bad people, laughter and tears. So it is on a pilgrimage. Like life, traveling is unpredictable, but we must persist until we reach our destination, be it the holy city of Jerusalem or the heavenly city of God. We are all pilgrims, even if we never leave home."

Hildegard looks directly at Margery. "You have spoken wisely, Margery. I never went on pilgrimage and yet, as you say, we are all journeying to eternal life. You have me thinking about my own journeys in my time as abbess. God showed me the way forward, but still I would sometimes succumb to doubt. In my later years, for example, God called me to set out on 'preaching tours,' even though that was a phrase that was not applied to women then. I was reluctant, not because I feared to speak out about the great insights God had given me, nor about the corruption and degradation that I had witnessed firsthand in the clergy of the day, but because of the continuing demands of my abbatial duties and (in truth) the aging of my body. Like you, Margery, I was determined, because it was my duty to honor God in this way and I accepted that aching bones and arthritic joints were just part and parcel of the journey. Mind you, these bodily ailments were exacerbated by my mode of travel—horses, and sometimes carts, all over the Rhineland and into Swabia, for the better part of 1160 when I was sixty-two years old. And, unlike what I've heard some say now, sixty was not the 'new forty' in the twelfth century."

"What about you Julian? Did you travel before you entered your anchorhold?" I ask.

"I cannot say much about the events of the earlier part of my life, I'm afraid,"[4] she replies and, as had happened previously, I notice Hildegard raising an index finger to her lips to advise me not to pursue this topic with Julian.

Cloud saves me from embarrassment by saying, lightly, "I think that Julian, like Richard and me, was very content with a life of solitude. That does not mean, of course, that we had no communication with others. As you know, already, I acted as spiritual advisor to young aspirants to the contemplative life. And you've heard that Julian spent many hours giving counsel to visitors (like Margery) at her anchorhold window. As for Richard, he, too, has told us about acting as spiritual guide for local anchoresses."

"Yes, thank you, Cloud," agrees Richard. "You express it well. I loved the solitary life in which I could spend my hours, uninterrupted, in God's love. It is not for everyone and, do not be mistaken, it was a demanding life—physically limited, spiritually, mentally, and emotionally draining at times; but, then, what mode of life isn't? And, as Cloud has explained, there were opportunities for communication with others. In fact, it was part of the calling. But pilgrimage and traveling more widely were not part of the solitary life."

Francis, looking wistful, shares, saying "I, too, despite my wandering and preaching, loved the solitary life and, when possible, I would go to one of the hermitages that were available to our friars. These were simple habitations, usually rough huts of branches and reeds, or similar, and always in lonely, wild places where I could let my soul soar."

---

4. There is no biographical information on Julian beyond that which she gives in her texts. These scant details, as covered already in this book, are limited to her childhood desire to be dedicated to God.

"One such place was La Verna, was it not, Francis?" asks Julian.

"Yes, one of the places dearest to my heart. It was a remote mountain, gifted to our order by Count Orlando Catani of Chiusi."

"And Francis, was it not there that you received the stigmata?" Julian's voice is quiet but her question draws my eyes to Francis's hands and wrists, and I notice, for the first time this evening that, beyond the wrist cuffs of his sweater, both hands are covered to the knuckles; he is wearing flesh-colored fingerless mittens of a very light material, not unlike the arthritis gloves that I've seen about.

"Yes again, Julian," replies Francis. "I had taken myself there from late August to early September 1224 for a forty-day fast. On the feast of the Exaltation of the Cross, I prayed for two graces: first, that during my life, I would experience, in my own body and soul, the pain that Christ experienced during the Passion; and second, that I could endure the pain, as Christ did, with great love for all sinners. I realized that these graces were to be granted because, as my prayer continued, I was swept up in an ecstasy during which a seraph with flaming wings prepared me for the change that was to come to me. Christ then appeared in this same seraphic vision, and I received the five wounds of the Passion—on my hands, my feet, and an opening in my right side. And then, when the vision vanished, I felt the great flame of love in my heart."

"A truly miraculous experience, Francis. It's said that you were the first person to receive the stigmata." This is not a question on Richard's part; it is a statement of fact.

Francis merely nods in response, and I wonder if the receipt of such wounds is too miraculous an occurrence to elaborate on. I decide not to press him for more details, and instead I ask him something about else that has fascinated me. "It's also said that you are responsible for initiating the celebration of the Nativity in a way that we honor and replicate to this very day."

"Annie, I happily and humbly claim my role in that. In my heart, I had always held a very great love of the feast of Christmas, because it was the remembrance and celebration of a lowly birth that changed the world. I wanted to honor the humility of Christ's birth in a manger in a Bethlehem stable for its simultaneous simplicity and greatness. Thus, around Christmastide 1223, the idea came to me that my brothers and I should recreate the scene of the nativity and, in it, we should make the central feature the baby in a manger, surrounded by animals, watched over by Mary and Joseph and attended by visiting shepherds and wise men. This scene became important enough to my brothers that they repeated a nativity scene at the Christmas Mass each year following its introduction. And, by God's grace, the practice persisted and spread."

"It certainly has persisted," I say. "It's a tradition that's loved by adults as well as children today. And, your inclusion of the animals in the scene, your love of animals . . . that's what people particularly associate with you, Francis."

"And who would not love animals?" Francis laughs and, as if on cue, Pat appears from under the coffee table and attempts to leap onto Francis's lap, upsetting the bowl with its remaining apple tart that was balancing there. The bowl and its contents fall onto the floor and Pat, suddenly torn between his rush of affection for Francis and his addiction to food, lets the addiction win and is scoffing down the remains of the tart from the living room floor before I've even registered exactly what's happening.

"Pat," I cry, "When did you sneak into the room?" I know that my annoyed voice is only spurring Pat on to eat more quickly, to gobble every last morsel—no thought to chewing any of it—before he's ordered back to the kitchen.

Francis bends down to pick up the bowl, which is by now licked clean, and with a wide smile says, "He might as well stay now, don't you think? He's cleaned up everything, so no harm done." And to my mixed annoyance and amusement, I see Pat looking up at me with the same plaintive expression that Francis has adopted. Silently, I admit defeat . . . and Pat and Francis know it. I settle back in my armchair and decide to enjoy the wonder of having Saint Francis of Assisi as an admirer of my dog.

As if picking up on my thoughts, Richard chuckles. "You tamed the Wolf of Gubbio so Pat's no challenge at all."

"Oh yes. Could you please share that story, Francis?" I ask. "And the one about preaching to the birds?"

"Listen carefully, Pat. You might learn something," Francis laughs as he smooths the fur around Pat's neck. "I was spending some time in Gubbio, a town in Umbria, not far from Assisi, when I became aware that the inhabitants were being terrorized by a large wolf. I felt very sorry that they were frightened, but I also felt for the animal so, despite the fears that the local people had for my safety, I decided to seek out the wolf and speak to him. With the townspeople following at a short distance, I set out in search of him. It didn't take long. He saw me first and went to lunge at me, sharp teeth bared. I held up my hand and said clearly, 'In the name of Jesus Christ, calm yourself, brother Wolf. Harm no one here.' Then, I made the sign of the cross and the animal approached me and, as gently as a lamb, sat at my side. I admonished him further saying, 'Brother Wolf, you have inflicted fear and anguish on this town by devouring other creatures and even attacking the townsfolk. You are commanded to stop.' And it was clear in the way that the wolf hung his head and tucked in his tail that he was sorry and subdued. I knew, however, that he was also hungry and so I made a pact with him. I explained that, if he promised never again to harm any creature, the people of the town would make sure that he was well fed every day for the rest of his life. His eyes told me that he understood, and he lifted his paw to rest it in my hand and we shook on the agreement. I used this experience as the basis for my preaching to those gathered around to see this spectacle, reminding them that the fires of hell are incalculably more fearsome than the jaws of a wolf and that it behooves them all to shun sin and love God. And so it was that Brother Wolf and the townsfolk each kept their side of the bargain with the wolf, who became a greatly loved member of the town. Even the town's dogs welcomed him."

Pat is sitting up now, ears pricked.

"Looks like Pat enjoyed the story as much as we humans did. And now that you've calmed Pat, too, could I offer you some more apple tart? At least a little replacement piece for what you lost to my dog," I suggest and, glancing around the room, I add, "And anyone else, while I'm at it?"

Francis agrees to another slice, and Richard follows his lead, but the others politely decline. They just look very content in the cozy circle we have created around the fireplace. Francis tilts his head at me when I insist that he needs a fresh bowl for the second helping, then he roars with laughter when I say, "Pat licked that bowl all over. You don't want dog germs."

"I don't know about germs," confides Julian, "but I do know that animals have played a special part in my life. I had a cat in my anchorhold to keep the mice under control.[5] She was pleasant company and lived to a fine old age. I grew very fond of her. And, still on the subject of animals, don't forget about the story of the birds, Francis," she prompts. "Of course, after you've finished your dessert."

"I've finished it. Too good to dawdle over," he says, holding up the newly empty bowl for all to see and then stretching to place it on the coffee table, well out of Pat's way. "Ah, the birds. They are very dear to me. However, it's not much of a story, really. Such as it is, it happened that I came to a point in my life where I longed to devote myself more fully to prayer, and yet I also had a feeling that God's plan for me involved more preaching. I prayed on this question and also asked advice from some trusted brothers and sisters. Very quickly and definitely they saw that my preaching should continue and so I hurried off to carry out God's directive. As I went on my way across a broad field, a huge flock of birds of every kind gathered on the trees and grass around me. And so I knew that I should preach to the birds. I told them about God's kind care of them in providing their clothing of warm feathers and the wonderful means of transport that their wings gave them. Among them was cause for much joy and gratitude at God's love. I blessed them with the sign of the cross and then bade them to go on their way. And they did, and so did I, all of us the happier for having had time together."

"Animals, like everything in God's creation—animate and inanimate—are deserving of care and respect." Hildegard's voice is authoritative. "I knew it in the twelfth century

---

5. Julian does not make any reference in her texts to having a cat. However, it is known that it was quite common for anchoresses, in general, to keep a cat to control mice in their anchorholds.

and I know it now: all of creation is a song of praise to God. The earth and all that is in it sustains humanity, and we, as humans, have the responsibility, in turn, to sustain the earth. It must not be destroyed; it must not be desecrated."

Her words strike a deep chord within me. "Hildegard, your warning is timely, or, I fear, probably too late. Our planet is in dire straits with global warming, melting polar areas, rising sea levels, and the extinction of many of our most precious species of plants, animals, and insects by overdevelopment for human habitation, the destruction of forests, the overfishing of our seas, those same seas choked with plastic refuse. And much of it is down to greed—of some wealthy countries taking everything and anything they want, because they have the money to do it."

"Yes, I know of this. It is not just tragic; it is against God's plan. Since the beginning of creation, God gave humans stewardship of the earth. Remember, God said, 'Let us make humankind in our image, in our likeness, so that they may rule over the fish in the sea and the birds in the sky, over the livestock and all the wild animals, and over all the creatures that move along the ground' (Gen 1:26). And stewardship is essentially about responsibility for protecting and preserving the great gift of creation that God has given us. I note that many people and agencies are trying to live up to this responsibility,[6] but there is so much more to be done."

---

6. At the turn of this current millennium Pope John Paul II made the point that "Humanity is no longer the Creator's 'steward' but an autonomous despot, who is finally beginning to understand that he must stop at the edge of the abyss. We must therefore stimulate and sustain the ecological conversion. . . . At stake is not only a 'physical' ecology that is concerned to safeguard the habitat of various living beings, but also a 'human' ecology which makes the existence of creatures more dig-

"Hildegard, earlier you explained briefly your idea of *viriditas.* Can you say a little more about it now, in relation to the importance of caring for our planet?" I hear the plaintive note in my voice.

"Of course, Annie," Hildegard replies graciously. "As I've said earlier, *viriditas* is, more or less, about the new, green shoots of possibility in our spirit as well as in nature. It's the potential, and the actuality, of growth, and the hope of renewal. We have our being in God; God is life itself, and thus, everything in nature is shot through with *viriditas*, with generative possibility. It follows that nature, and everything in creation, is alive with God. And God remains beyond time and throughout eternity. In my *Book of Divine Works*, I relate, as I was shown, that eternity is called the Father, the Word is called the Son, and the breath that connects these two is called the Holy Spirit. This interconnection of the Trinity is reflected in the whole of creation so that everything has meaning and everything is connected to everything else and, most importantly, to God. Therefore, we cannot fail to care for the very least thing in God's creation because everything is of significance, everything is loved."

"The smallest thing shall not be forgotten," intones Julian. "That was what I was shown. It behooves us to care for everything, as you are saying, Hildegard."

"Precisely, Julian." Hildegard gives a quick clap of her hands. "I understood the principle of 'as above, so below'

nified, by protecting the fundamental good of life in all its manifestations and by preparing for future generations an environment closer to the plan of the Creator" (Pope John Paul II, General Audience, January 17, 2001); Pope Francis's encyclical letter on ecology and climate, *Laudato Si'* (2015), takes up and details the current problems and responsibilities of caring for our earthly home.

very well, and it became the guide for all my work in natural science and medicine. That is, we believed that the four elements of earth, fire, water, and air were present not only in the great planet and (known) universe in which we dwelt in the twelfth century but in each and every living and inanimate thing within that universe. Not just present, everything within our world and within humans and animals and plants and rocks—everything that we knew of then—was composed of various combinations of these elements and of what we called their contraries: *cold*, *hot*, *moist*, and *dry*. Contraries were the inherent properties of the elements. If you think about it, even now, it's obvious that the element of water would have the contraries of 'moist' and 'cold'; and you might guess that fire would be 'hot' and 'dry'; that means that the earth element is 'dry' and 'cold'; leaving air to have the contraries of 'hot' and 'moist.' In addition, combinations of any two of the contraries produced in each and every person one of four main *complexions* (also called *temperaments*) and an accompanying predominant bodily fluid (*humor*). For example, the combination of hot and moist contraries resulted in a *sanguine* temperament and a predominance of blood in the system; hot and dry contraries produced a *choleric* temperament and a predominance of yellow bile; a cold and dry combination resulted in a *melancholic* temperament and an accompanying abundance of black bile; while a cold and moist mixture produced a *phlegmatic* individual, who was in possession of a generous amount of phlegm.

"In every person, there was a little of all the elements and contraries, so that when it came to treating medical problems and illnesses, we physicians would look to the predominant humor and temperament of the individual. That was because we understood illness to be a disturbance in a patient's predominating *humor*, and treatment aimed, therefore, at restoring the humoral balance. Usually, this treatment utilized the 'like-cures-like' approach, which meant using herbs or other natural means that were similar in their intrinsic properties to the patient's own contraries and predominating humor. Thus, it was also necessary to know the properties of the herbs we were using. There is a treatment in nature for every illness, you know, because God has given us everything in creation for our use and betterment."

"Could you give some examples of illnesses and their treatments, Hildegard?" I ask.

"Hildegard, please, some help with my gout," Richard pleads.

"That is an easy one, Richard. Cinnamon is what you need. Take it sprinkled on bread or make it into a tea.

"What about something for a bit of queasiness, especially when I'm nervous?" Margery asks. "I suffer from that quite often...a lingering problem from my days on pilgrimage when I had to eat in some inns of very questionable quality."[7]

"Margery, you will benefit from cumin, and I suggest you make use of it in cookies for easy consumption when the mood and need takes you. What you do is mix a powder of cumin with pure wheat flour, an egg yolk and a little water. Shape the mix into cookies and bake in a hot oven, and eat as needed."

---

7. Hildegard's herbal recommendations presented here have been creatively interpreted and/or modified by the author. For the complete details of Hildegard's extensive medicinal recommendations see, for example: Hildegard of Bingen, *Hildegard von Bingen's Physica: The Complete English Translation of Her Classic Work on Health and Healing*, trans. Priscilla Throop, (Rochester, NY: Healing Arts Press, 1998).

"So helpful, Hildegard," says Richard, who has taken a small notepad from his shirt pocket and is jotting down the recommendations as they come. "What else?"

"Well, let me think. I don't want to take up the whole evening with this. My medical writings are quite extensive, you know. Perhaps some basic, general advice could be worthwhile.[8] Umm…alright. Chervil, a bit of garlic and sage with vinegar, prepared as a condiment, is good for those with a poor appetite."

"I don't think any of us here need that one, Hildegard," laughs Cloud.

"Quite right," agrees Hildegard, very readily. "Well, what about an ointment of sage, oregano, fennel, and butter applied to the head—very effective for a headache?" Hildegard looks across at me and enquires, "What can I help you with, Annie. You look worried."

"No, no, not worried, Hildegard. I was just thinking about what happened earlier with Margery. I saw you put something in her mouth. And then I saw you, Margery, remove something quite soon afterwards. I was wondering if that was one of your special treatments."

"Indeed it was," asserts Hildegard. She reaches into her pocket, as she had done earlier with Margery, and brings out what looks like a small, shiny stone. She passes it to me. I look carefully at it on my palm. It is brilliant green and very beautiful.

"It's lovely. It looks like some kind of jewel," I say, hearing my own confusion.

---

8. Note that Hildegard's remedies given here are in no way recommended as treatments for medical issues today.

"Correct, Annie. It's an emerald. As we've discussed, God has made everything for our use, and the stones of the Earth—all of which are composed of fire and water—are particularly useful for many ailments. For someone like Margery, who suffers from the falling sickness, our medieval approach was to place an emerald in the mouth after the subject was awake, but still prostrate, and leave it there for a short time because it has the effect of reviving the spirit."

"Not many people today have an emerald in their pocket," I laugh.

"Yes, I know this to be true. But, when gemstones were available, they were considered powerful aids in returning people to health."

Margery is enjoying this conversation, adding her own anecdote: "On my travels, I heard of the most miraculous healings involving what was known as *manuschristi*—the hand of Christ. Fellow pilgrims told me of the Dominican monks of Bologna who were also widely known for the excellence of their remedies. Their most frequently prepared cure, to be ingested by the sufferer, was this famous *manuschristi*, which was a confection of crushed pearls, gold, rosewater, chopped lemon, spices, marzipan, and sugar."

"Hmmm. Don't really have any crushed pearls around here," I say, my eyes wide at the thought.

"No, even then, it was a treatment for those who had wealth. Sugar didn't come cheap!" Hildegard winks at me. "But something green, and not too expensive, which is more readily available is the apple. Apples were a staple medicine wherever they were available. When cooked, they were considered to be very beneficial for sick persons in general, while a salve made from apple leaves was regarded as being especially good for the eyes. So, an excellent choice for our dessert tart, Annie."

"Ha, a happy coincidence! But that's something green that I have in the kitchen at all times," I say. "No doubt this earlier medicinal use of apples is part of the basis for our present-day saying, 'an apple a day keeps the doctor away.'"

The guests take a moment to chat about apples and pearls and the wonder of God's creation, and I take a moment to mull over a question that has come to my mind regarding Hildegard's amazing knowledge of the natural world.

Hildegard turns her head in my direction. "Once again, Annie, I see that you are thinking about something. You look a little uneasy. But we're all friends here. What is it you want to ask?"

I take a breath. "Hildegard, it is more or less common knowledge now that you were the first person to describe the female orgasm."

"Absolutely right, Annie. And why would you hesitate to ask me that? It is perfectly natural, part of God's wonderful plan. My nuns and I assisted many women in childbirth and all that was associated with that. In discussion with many of them, I came to understand that the woman had a very particular role in the act of procreation. Her physical response was important. It is never just about the man, you know."

"I think we should drink to that," says Margery. And Francis goes quickly to the dining room and then back, bringing in the bottle of wine and the jug of water we had left there on the table in our hurry to settle Margery after her falling incident. Cloud has followed and reappears with glasses which are soon filled with people's choice of beverage, and we raise our glasses to Hildegard's toast of "Here's to God's creation, full of wonders, in every way."

Francis takes his glass with him to stand closer to the fire. He then turns his back toward the warmth so that he is facing all of us. I can tell that he is thinking deeply about something. The others pick up on it, too, and the general conversation stops in expectation of what Francis has to say. We are not disappointed.

"It was, and still is, a source of considerable surprise and disappointment to me, that women are not properly recognized for their valuable role in the world—material and religious. All people are equal in God's eyes. In 1212, I had the privilege of meeting Clare, a young noblewoman of Assisi. Apparently, she had heard me preaching on the embrace of God via a simple life of poverty, and she was stirred in her heart to do the same. And why would God not inspire women? I had no hesitation in helping her into a form of Minorite life with its attendant poverty, penance, and seclusion but, of course, it was necessary for her to stay for a time with the Benedictine nuns until I could find an appropriate retreat for her and her sister, Agnes, and other young female companions who had joined them, desiring also to follow the life. This group of admirable women became the founding members of what came to be known as the Second Franciscan Order of Poor Ladies (or, as you might know them, the Poor Clares). Clare and I were spiritual friends and, in times of difficulty or anguish, I would often seek her prayers and advice. Such was the case when, in the last year of my life, my body was frail and my eyesight was failing, its decline having been hastened, unfortunately, by a painful treatment I had undergone. It involved having my temples cauterized in the hope that my eyesight might be restored and the pain relieved. The treatment achieved neither objective. And it was at this low point that I paid a last visit to my friend. As far as I recall, this was in late 1225, and thanks be to God and to the prayers and kind encouragement of my dear sister, Clare, I took brief refuge in a small reed-covered hut in the sisters' garden in San Damiano. It was there that I composed the song that many people, down to the present day, associate with me: the *Canticle of the Sun*."

"It's a wonderful prayer, Francis. And you're absolutely right that many today know it or, at least, know of it," I agree. "In some ways, it's become an important reminder for us now to respect and be grateful for everything in creation—just as we were talking about a little earlier." I pause for a moment, a smile playing on my lips, before saying, "I think you know what I'm going to ask you."

"No need to ask, Annie. As I said earlier, what were my brothers and I but God's minstrels! I am delighted to sing a little of the canticle for you all."

And with that, Francis's clear baritone voice fills the living room and, for the first time, I hear the original melody of this famous canticle, as well as its words, straight from the composer himself. I am enthralled as Francis sings:

> Praised be You, my Lord, with all Your crea-
>   tures,
> especially worshipful Brother Sun,
> Who lights up the day and through whom You
>   give us brightness.
> And he is beautiful and radiant and splendid,
> and reflects the likeness of You, Most High
>   One.
>
> Praised be You, my Lord, for Sister Moon and
>   the stars in heaven.

You have formed them clear and precious and
    beautiful.

Praised be You, my Lord, for Brother Wind,
and for the air, cloudy and serene, and every
    kind of weather,
through whom You give sustenance to Your
    creatures.

Praised be You, my Lord, for Sister Water,
who is very useful and humble and precious and
    pure.

Praised be You, my Lord, for Brother Fire
through whom You light the night,
and he is beautiful and playful and robust and
    strong.

Praised be You, my Lord, for our Sister Mother
    Earth
who sustains and governs us,
and who produces various fruit with colored
    flowers and herbs.[9]

Francis ends his presentation there with a little bow, and
we break into spontaneous applause. He holds up his hands
in mock-imitation of someone silencing a large crowd, and

---

9. *The Canticle of the Sun*, like all of Francis's writings, is in the public domain. This translated version is from the Assisi MS. 338 (fol. 33) which can be found at https://en.wikisource.org/wiki/The_Writings_of_St._Francis_of_Assisi/The_Canticle_of_the_Sun.

we comply as he continues, "There is another verse to that song which pertains to 'our Sister, bodily Death,' and it is fitting that we praise God for death as it rounds out our life in time and brings us to life in divine eternity. As it happened, that final verse became relevant to me just a year after the composition of the canticle. For now, however, I'd like go back to my opening reflection on the importance of women in every aspect of life and, thus, to end my little performance with a tribute to Clare, who prayed and worked tirelessly to gain papal approval for the Order of the Poor Clares, until permission was finally given on August 11, 1253, two days before her death. Now that is faith and hope in action. And it has nothing to do with whether one is male or female."

It's easy to see that the group is in total agreement with Francis. A quiet interval follows before they are nodding to each other and a few one-to-one chats are starting up. Seeing my guests so relaxed and comfortable, I think about clearing the empty dessert plates from the coffee table but quickly change my mind when Julian speaks. "Hildegard, your explanation of everything having a meaning—every material thing linked to a spiritual meaning—found a particular resonance with me. It was certainly the case when I had cause to meditate on some of the more complex aspects of my initial showings."

"I would like to hear more, Julian," says Hildegard, eyes bright in expectation.

"Very well. You recall, I'm sure, how I told you earlier that I was especially troubled by the issue of sin during my revelations. And this disquiet continued in my prayer life long after the showings were completed; for although I had received divine answers to every query I had posed, and most lovingly so, I still wondered how we humans could continue to fail in our love of God when God's love never fails us. As you might also know, the accounts of my revelations exists in two forms. The first is what is now commonly known as the *Short Text*, which I wrote immediately after my revelatory experience, to ensure that all intrinsic and miraculous details were preserved while my memory was fresh. In truth, I need not have worried about my memory of those showings staying fresh because the richness of my experience remained with me, in vivid detail, for the rest of my life. Most importantly, the showings formed the basis of my prayer and meditation from then on; and guided by the Holy Spirit—just as if I had been a child being taught my spiritual ABCs—I found the full depth of meaning of all that I had received on that day in May 1373. And so it happened that about twenty years after I wrote the Short Text, I was called to write an extended version, in which God enabled me to share the full import of all with which I had been blessed and entrusted. This version is now usually referred to as the *Long Text* and it is there that I revealed one aspect of the initial experience that, at the time of writing my Short Text, I was not able to comprehend at all. However, I knew, without doubt, that it was very important, and so, for many years, I had prayed for the guidance to share it adequately. This component is what is called generally today the 'Lord and Servant' allegory. And, when you were talking of everything having a significance, Hildegard, I thought of this allegory, as I often do, and of how I was shown, over the years, the meaning of every aspect of that part of my fourteenth revelation. Of course, it is neither the time nor the place for me to go through every detail, but the broad significance might be helpful because, despite the great mercy and love which God assured me was ours throughout all my revelations, I still could not reconcile this with the Church's teachings and the persistence of our human failings."

"Allegories are most helpful as a means of presenting complex matters in an accessible way," says Hildegard. "After all, Jesus often spoke in parables."

"Quite so," agrees Julian. "And I was led to realize that my own lack of understanding—and in this, I represent all humans, the one standing for all—is part of the very reason that God is so merciful to us. You see, in the vision I had seen two people, one clearly a powerful and wealthy man, a lord over others; the second, a humble but devoted servant of the great lord. The lord, who loved the servant for his diligence and desire to please, called the servant to him and instructed him to set out on an important errand. The servant was delighted to oblige his lord and happily hurried off to carry out the lord's bidding. In his haste, he failed to notice a wide and deep ditch in the road, and, thus, fell into the ditch and injured himself badly, so badly, in fact, that he was unable to get himself out, and unable to turn his face to look up and realize that his lord was there, quite nearby, seeking to help him. In so much pain was the servant that he almost forgot the lord and the task with which he had been entrusted. But the lord knew of the servant's good will and fervent desire to please him . . . and he knew the servant would have done so, if he had not fallen; and so the lord apportioned no blame to the servant for his inability to complete the errand but, instead, only loved him for his efforts. In my meditation over the years, I was to see that the lord of the allegory was God, and the servant was Adam who, like the servant, first fell and lost clear remembrance of his lord (God) and of the task he had been set. At a deeper level, I came to understand that the servant also represents Jesus who 'fell' into a maiden's womb and, thus, into life; and thus the servant, and Adam, and Jesus—the 'second Adam'—represent us all in our humanity and in our 'falling,' though, of course, Jesus's fall was not one of failing, as were the falls of the servant and Adam. There are more complex things to be said about this, but the most important thing is that, just as Jesus Christ, the second person of the Trinity, 'fell' into life, he did so to raise us all from the ditch by his own resurrection, and, therefore in God's view—which, of course is also the 'view' of Jesus Christ as the second person of the Trinity—no blame applies to us, but only mercy and love."

"This is a very hopeful message, Julian." Hildegard is furrowing her brows and I am wondering if she disapproves of Julian's conclusion, until she says, "And it's a message that is absolutely in line with everything I know of God's love."

Cloud is mulling over something too, I see. "Hmmm. Yes. Yes Julian. I appreciate your elaboration of this allegory. It aligns with my understanding that a good will is the substance of finding one's way to God. When we are in that space between the cloud of forgetting and the cloud of unknowing, we are not unlike the servant. Our only option is to try and strike through the cloud with that dart of love I've already spoken about."

"And I have written quite often in my texts for those dedicated anchoresses for whom I took the role of spiritual advisor that love is the ardent yearning for God—note, not necessarily the attainment but, as Cloud says, the intention to attain," contributes Richard.

"Richard, I know that you've written about this yearning and of God's great mercy in some of your lyrics, too," says Margery. "Can you share any of those?"

"Ah, snippets only," Richard smiles. "I think we have been given the most wonderful lyrics tonight in Francis's beautiful canticle. And, as it happens, I am keen to hear of your music, Hildegard, which, unlike my poems—and here, I am being honest, no false modesty—have stood the test of time.[10] But, as you've asked, Margery—and here I have to confess that the lyrics are not even that memorable for me, their composer—I'll give you a tiny sample from a longer poem on God's mercy and love which echoes the point that I stressed to the anchoresses about longing:

> My song is in sighing, whilst I dwell in this way,
> My life is a longing that binds night and day
> Till I come to my King to dwell with him I may
> And I see his fair shining in life that lasts
>   for aye."[11]

"It's catchy," says Margery. "I like the rhyme, and that certainly helps with the memory. It's now in my head and I shall enjoy reciting it as a little prayer of longing."

"You are too kind, Margery. But if it's of any use, I'm gratified. Now, Hildegard, please can we talk about your music?"

"There's not much to say, Richard, other than that I composed my music and accompanying lyrics for the express purpose of praising God. In my compositions, I favored melodies and words that soared upward, lifting the soul heavenward. But, in the twelfth century, musical notation was limited, showing no tempo or rhythm, and thus my music

---

10. In the century following Richard Rolle's death (c. 1349), his English writings, including his lyrics, became very popular, but their popularity decreased markedly after that time.

11. Richard Rolle, "Lyrics," in *Richard Rolle: Prose and Verse*, ed. S. J. Ogilvie-Thomson, EETS, no. 293 (Oxford: Oxford University Press, 1988), 44.

was based on monophonic plainchant with the addition of ornamental neumas to extend the effect and variation. My nuns and I would sing the compositions with great enthusiasm during our many liturgies in the abbey."

"Hildegard, you do realize that you are frequently included on lists of the greatest composers of all times, don't you?" I ask.

Hildegard shrugs her shoulders in response.

"And," I press on, "modern productions of your *Canticles of Ecstasy* and *Voices of Angels*, each have around two million views on YouTube—as of last time I checked—and climbing. Not to mention millions of downloads from music-streaming services."

"Music has the ability to touch people," Hildegard says simply.

I long to know more and so I ask, "You wrote a musical play, too. Was that unusual in your day?"

"As a matter of fact, it *was* unusual, and actually quite original in that it was not composed to be part of a liturgy. That was in 1151 and it was titled *Ordo Virtutum* ('Play of the Virtues'). In style, it was an allegorical morality play which depicted the Christian story of sin, repentance, and forgiveness. It contained eighty-two original songs, so I suppose, perhaps, I could take credit for writing the earliest known musical drama—though with a sacred theme."

"Did it have characters? Who were the performers?" I ask excitedly as the whole idea of a musical written by an abbess in 1151 is really firing up my imagination.

"Well now, let me think," replies Hildegard and she does, indeed, close her eyes for a few moments as if in deep thought. "I recall that the characters included patriarchs, a few prophets, a happy soul, and an unhappy soul. And there were, from memory, the personification of sixteen female Virtues that included Mercy, Innocence, Obedience, Chastity, Hope, Faith, and so on. The performers of all these roles were women: nuns of our Rupertsberg convent and a few other local noblewomen. The women presented their parts in Latin, singing in the monophonic plainchant of the day. And, you might be surprised to know that there was one male in the cast—my secretary and spiritual advisor, Volmar. He played the devil and, as such, he did not have a singing part but, instead, was limited to shouts and screams." Hildegard looks around at us all and suddenly roars with laughter. "He was very effective in that role."

We all laugh with her but her eyes fix on me as she asks, "I believe there is something else you want to know, Annie."

Sheepishly, I acknowledge that she is right...again. "There is, Hildegard," I admit. "I'm just wondering about all the magnificent images that feature along with the words in your visionary trilogy."

"Easy, quick answer, Annie. It's usually thought, by historians and the like, that I did not personally 'draw' and color any of them but that, as all the images certainly are accurate and fully detailed depictions of the visions as I've described them, it is probable that I orchestrated and supervised the production of the illuminations by my nuns in the convent scriptorium. Who am I to disagree with experts at this late stage?" Hildegard leans back in her chair and folds her arms.

My guests are shooting me wry smiles, and I cannot help but respond in kind. Still, I take it as a sign that this part of our conversation has come to a natural conclusion and I stand up, ready to get the dessert bowls out of the way and head for the kitchen to make coffee or tea or whatever the guests might enjoy next.

Francis stands with me and I think he is going to offer to help in the kitchen again but, instead, he says, "Before you clear the dishes away, Annie, I have a gift for you. It's a very tiny gift but now seems like the moment to offer it to you. It's my way of saying thank you for the beautiful meal and very special evening that we have shared." He waves away my attempt to respond and continues, "You have heard my *Canticle of the Sun* tonight. Humbly, I have composed another canticle; and this one is in honor of your wonderful hospitality, Annie. It is intended as a memento for you, and so I wrote and recorded it earlier in the day, and arranged with one of my very technologically clever brothers—at least, in comparison to me—to send it to your phone during this evening. I believe it will have arrived by now and you may listen to it at your leisure. There is no need to share it, if you would rather not."

I am astounded. How did Francis arrange such a thing? I am adamant that I want to listen and to share it with everyone, immediately. "Please excuse me for a moment," I call back to my guests as I hurry to retrieve my phone from the charger in the kitchen. As I take up the phone I see that, sure enough, a sound file has appeared. I rush back to the living room and download the file which I now see is entitled *Canticle of Dinner*. With the volume at maximum, we listen to Francis's clear voice once again singing:

Praised be You, my Lord, through Brother
    Salmon, baked to perfection
And with all accompaniments
Especially Sir Brother Lemon-butter sauce
Who adds the finishing touch to your great and
    delectable splendor.

Praised be You, my Lord, through Sister Barley,
and through the spinach and mushrooms
that enhance the tastiness in this cool
weather,
And through whom You give sustenance to
those at dinner.

Praised be You, my Lord, through Brother
Apple Tart who is delicate and delicious,
And deserving of a second helping (with
cinnamon cream).

Praised be You, my Lord, through Sister Annie,
through whom You light our night,
and who has welcomed us with open arms
and heart.

I know I am holding back happy tears as I struggle to say, "Thank you, Francis." I do not even begin to imagine how Francis knew before his arrival what the menu would be. In truth, I had dithered about aspects of it until this morning. I stand in wonder for several minutes before rousing myself to gather up the dessert things and float out to the kitchen to prepare for the next part of the evening.

Coffee

The mystics' insights that may be relevant to the world of the twenty-first century are presented and discussed.

Outside the warm kitchen, the yard is getting lashed by heavy rain, and a furious wind is tearing smaller branches from the trees and slamming them into the grass or bouncing them off the garden furniture. Inside the warm kitchen, I'm humming Francis's "Canticle of Dinner" as I set the coffee press on the tray next to a pot of black tea and one of peppermint tea. Cups, teaspoons, a jug of milk, a sugar bowl. . . . I check off the list in my head, making sure I have everything we'll need.

"Don't forget the glasses that Hildegard asked you to bring in," comes a voice from behind me.

It's Julian, serene and smiling. "I thought it was about time I helped you. It's been such a special evening." She steps closer and I notice—as I had when she arrived—her smooth skin, almost translucent.

"Thank you, Julian. There's not much to do, but you're correct about needing the glasses. I'm not sure why Hildegard has requested them but she did say small glasses would be best, so I think liqueur glasses will do, don't you?"

"Definitely," she agrees. "Much neater and easier to manage. Shall I get them for you?"

"Over there." I point to the corner cupboard. "Third shelf, on the right."

She finds them easily and crosses the kitchen to put them on the tray. "I really mean it, Annie," she says quietly. "This dinner party has been a joy for me. I don't get out much and, I admit, I was quite nervous about the idea. Oh, yes, it's true that, in the end, I was the one persuading Margery out of her cozy cottage and into the rain for us to make the trip here. But as you've seen, Margery is in her element in company, whereas I . . . I'm a bit shy. And I know I can sound rather serious in general conversation."

"Well, you've had some serious subject matter to share with us, Julian. And everything you've said has been fascinating. I can honestly say that I couldn't have wished for more interesting, diverse, and open-hearted guests than I have here tonight."

"You are very gracious, Annie."

I remain silent for a moment, thinking that she might have more to say but, instead, she steps back from the tray and stands still and upright, her fine-boned hands clasped together at waist-level. I presume that she is waiting for me to suggest how she might assist me, so I put my silence aside and say, "Julian, on the counter over there, you'll see a storage container with my special almond and hazelnut meringue cookies in it. If you don't mind, would you please choose a pretty serving plate from that corner cupboard, second shelf this time, and set the cookies on it. I'm just going to grab some small plates and then we're ready to go."

"When I've gotten those plates, Annie, why don't you go ahead and sit down with your guests? I'll organize the cookies and then bring them in with everything else on the tray."

"The tray will be very heavy, Julian. Perhaps I should help you by taking the coffee press with me," I suggest.

"Yes, do that, but leave all the rest. I'm stronger than I look," she laughs and, with a backward wave of her hand, directs me out of the kitchen. I obey and head for the living room where, as I expected, everyone is comfortably chatting and looking very relaxed in the warm glow of the fire. I put the small plates and the coffee on the low table and then I am immediately part of the circle again.

"Take a seat, Annie," calls Margery when she sees me. "We were just talking about memory and how fortunate we were in the Middle Ages to be able to depend on our own reliable memories for all sorts of information without recourse to . . . um . . . what's that thing called?"

"You mean the internet, Margery?" offers Francis.

"That's it. Google this and that. Amazing as it is—and it is amazing that, at the touch of buttons, all the information in the world is accessible—I sometimes wonder what would happen if the internet suddenly disappeared. I mean, how would people know anything about the past, or even the present? What do you think, Annie?"

"That's a very interesting question—and a scary prospect considering our reliance on the internet. The complete disappearance of online information would be world-changing, I think. Thank God we would still have libraries full of books and other resources. And maybe children would need to talk in more depth to their grandparents. And there's no doubt we'd need to sharpen up our memory skills."

"Well, of course, a good memory was essential in the Middle Ages," offers Julian. She has entered the room unnoticed until now, and is carrying the laden tray to the coffee table with no apparent effort. She places it down gently, half-turns to everyone, and continues speaking. "What I mean is that we had no choice but to remember. In medieval times, even though there were books, only the wealthy owned them. Perhaps someone like me, in my position of an enclosed anchoress, might have possessed a couple of precious handwritten books but, otherwise, anyone who was thirsty for knowledge had to listen carefully to any book that was read to them, and then memorize key words, phrases, whole sections for recall and reflection later on. If we needed to find our way in a new town we were visiting, we might ask a local for directions, and then, keeping the instructions in our memory, look for the signs and landmarks and so on as we went. And not necessarily just visual signs. For example, if I had to get to some establishment near the town's river, I would follow my nose because tanneries and other very odious—quite literally—businesses were always located on the riverside."

Cloud laughs and says, "Julian, you're absolutely right that we had very sharp memories then, but there wasn't as much to remember. There's great freedom and diversity of thoughts and ideas now. In our medieval lifetimes, a large proportion of the populace was illiterate, so important information had to be committed to memory. Trade skills were passed from master to apprentice by word of mouth, and by example into practice. The main stories of the Old Testament and the details of Jesus's birth, life, and death were learned by heart. Furthermore, the Church encouraged people to be well-schooled in the notion of 'reading' symbols. By that I mean that, as Hildegard has so eloquently explained to us this evening, so many things, so many details in the medieval world signified something else, most often something holy.

The sacred and the ordinary were inextricably intertwined in medieval understanding. Thus, while people could not read the Bible for themselves (and, that was not just because they were illiterate but also because Bibles were written in Latin, not vernacular languages, and additionally, because the Church hierarchy did not want 'ordinary' people interpreting scripture themselves), they could understand the symbolic language of the richly colored and ornate images in the stained-glass windows and the statues and paintings in churches and cathedrals, and the Bible stories filed in their memories reinforced their understanding. As you've pointed out, Julian, other senses also played a role in memory. For example, most people could not understand the Latin words of the Mass and other religious ceremonies, but they could 'read' the significance of the colors of the holy seasons, and they could even 'read' the sounds of bells and chants, and the smells of the incense used at various times."

I'm taking a mental note of everything Cloud is saying. "This is so interesting, Cloud. Your point about people using all the senses to understand the world and their religious lives shows me very clearly how Richard's *canor*, *calor*, and *dulcor*, for example, would have met with such enthusiasm at the time."

"You're right, Annie. We used all our senses in receiving our visions, all our senses in conveying our visions, and all our senses in memorizing and reflecting on our visions," explains Hildegard. "And, speaking of memory. . . ." Hildegard bends down to the side of her chair to retrieve the black leather satchel she has been carrying with her since she arrived. We watch as, with a flourish, she reaches into the bag and pulls out a brown earthenware vessel, roughly shaped like a bottle, and sealed with what looks like wax.

"This, my dears, is a special gift for us all to share. I'm sure you know that the Benedictine order of monks has long taken an interest in producing exceptional wines. And fortified wines like this one, too," she says, holding the bottle aloft, and then lowering it to unseal it, expertly.

Francis is up on his feet and pouring the dark golden liquid into each liqueur glass.

We raise our glasses in a toast, and I take a sip of the smoothest drink I have ever tasted.

"This is amazing, Hildegard. What sort of fortified wine is it, exactly?" I ask.

"I suppose you'd call it 'brandy' now, so let's just call it that."

"Did you say it came from an abbey of Benedictine monks?"

"No, I said that Benedictine monks are well-known for making exceptional wine and liqueurs. But this one is from an exceptional Benedictine abbey of an exceptional group of nuns who, by adding special herbs during the wine-making process, managed to perfect the skill of preserving wines for a very long time.[1] The nuns of my abbey in Rupertsberg, to be precise." She winks.

"But, Hildegard, that abbey... um... I've read that Rupertsberg didn't really continue for very long as an abbey after your... um... departure in 1179."

"That's correct, Annie. Nothing like a well-aged brandy, I always say. Drink up." Hildegard blesses me with one of her winks again.

---

1. This is a creative interpolation by the author. No records exist of Hildegard's abbey in Rupertsberg ever being involved in winemaking.

I'm stunned into silence at the thought of how old this excellent brandy must be, but the guests, as usual, take it in their stride as they help themselves to coffee or tea, and the meringue treats to accompany the fine liqueur. Again, I smile inwardly at the manner in which they've taken away all the stress of hosting a dinner.

Margery seems to have read my mind when she says, "I feel so comfortable here in your home, Annie. It's a lot grander than my tiny cottage, and, I admit, I do envy you a little having running water in the kitchen, glass in the windows, an internal bathroom, and electricity throughout, but there's real friendship and hospitality here."

"Yes, Margery speaks for all of us. It's heartening to know, even though years pass into centuries and life moves on, that friends can still gather for a lovely meal together," says Cloud, sipping on his brandy.

"You know that it's been my privilege to have you here. I've learned so much this evening about your lives and mystical experiences, and about your writings," I assure them and then, taking a deep breath, I continue, "And do you recall, at the start of the evening, I mentioned that I had wondered what you might say to us today, what advice you might give us, about meaning and purpose in life?"

Six heads are nodding in my direction.

"Yes, definitely. You know that we told you how good our memories were in the Middle Ages. They're still good enough to recall every detail of this evening," Richard says. With a smile he adds, "I know I speak for all: we're very happy to help in any way we can."

Hildegard has put her teacup down and is looking at me intently. "You see, as we've told you, it's important to us that we have shared God's gifts to us as thoroughly as possible. In our day, we wrote down our visions and insights and experiences for the benefit of all. But times change and, as we've talked about, the world of the twenty-first century is vastly different from the medieval world. But it is as it is for a reason, and we want to contribute appropriately to the here and now. Is there anything, in particular that we can help with, Annie?"

"Well, I think, if it's possible, that I'd like each one of you to share the main things that you learned from your life and mystical experiences," I respond. "You know, a sort of summary."

"Do you mean a 'How to be a Successful Mystic' sort of summary, Annie?" asks Francis, with a smile on his face.

I laugh and reply, "That might be really good. But, no, what you have to offer is serious; it can't be trivialized. I was just thinking that, as we've discussed so many things this evening, it would be good to have some key points to keep in mind."

"What you're asking us is very reasonable," reflects Hildegard. "I understand how crystallizing tonight's discussion into some essential points would be of benefit today. After all, if the Twitter limit is only two hundred and eighty characters for its users, I'm sure we can streamline our messages. Of course, even in our own day, there was difficulty in trying to honor God by the faithful delivery of our visions," Hildegard reassures me. "In other words, we had to express ourselves in a language that people could understand and so that meant approximating, diluting, the power and beauty of what we had seen and heard. Mystics see beyond the veil of everyday life to the greater reality, the true divine reality. There was and always will be a limit to our ability to share our insights, because the mystery and wonder of God cannot be anywhere near adequately rendered in language. By definition, if a mystery can be explained, then it's not a mystery."

"Very true, Hildegard," agrees Richard. "A mystery is not to be solved; it is to be embraced. But, as for streamlining the essentials of my experience, I'm happy to try."

Julian looks a little apprehensive as she says, "I might need a little time to get my thoughts in order but, yes, of course I'll do this for you, Annie."

"No rush, and no pressure," I say. "Perhaps, while you're all thinking about it and enjoying your coffee and brandy, I could give my own summary on some of the obvious signs of your influence today?"

"Sounds good," chirps Francis.

I don't see anyone disagreeing, so I make a start. "I want to do this to show you that people *are* really interested in you, interested to know about medieval mystics. They want to know what you have to say. It's the reason that your texts are still in print, readily available in libraries and bookstores. And that's remarkable, because, let's face it, you all lived and wrote a long time ago."

"We're like fine wine or brandy," says Margery.

"True. But you're not just being read, you're being studied and quoted," I emphasize.

"And Francis and Hildegard, you're both saints of the Church, and high profile saints, at that. Francis, I know you were canonized way back in 1228 and...." I pause to fumble again for the notes stashed in my pocket. "Excuse me, but I want to get this right. Ah, yes. So, in 1939, you were proclaimed a patron saint of Italy. And, of course, you're the patron saint of animals. Then, in 1980—a time when the world was becoming more aware of the terrible problems that our planet is facing because of abuse and misuse of natural resources—Pope John Paul II declared you the patron saint of ecology. That was a popular move, as was Jorge Bergoglio taking the name 'Francis' on being elected pope in 2013."

"That's a very positive sign, isn't it? It gives people hope that the Church will honor the idea of preferential treatment for the poor and intensify the commitment to care for planet Earth, among other things," reflects Richard.

"Definitely! And it's testimony to the high regard in which you're held, Francis. People of today certainly know about you—and your legacy," I say.

"Thank you, Annie, but it's not really my doing. It's God's; and my brother friars who have kept up the ideals and commitments of our original group over many centuries. Their work continues to speak today." Francis is sitting cross-legged on the floor, just to the side of the fireplace. Pat is sprawled next to him, hogging much of the fire's warmth while still managing to rest his head on Francis's knee.

"Still, Annie is right. It's a fine testament to you, Francis," insists Hildegard.

"You've left quite a testament yourself, Hildegard," I say, referring to my notes again and reading out the details: "You had been locally recognized as a saint since the twelfth century but, amazingly, you weren't officially canonized by the Church until May 2012 by Pope Benedict, and later that same year you were named a Doctor of the Church."

"Yes, one of only four female doctors, I believe, among the Church's thirty-five male doctors," Hildegard clarifies.

I nod and continue. "Plus, you're the unofficial patron saint of musicians and writers. Your music is readily available, as you know, but it's also performed quite often; and so is your play."

"All of these things are wonderful signs of interest in God's work through us, aren't they," comments Julian.

"Definitely," I reply. "And I think you'll all be pleased to know—following our earlier discussion on pilgrimage—that you are 'sites' for travelers today." I sneak another look at my notes and continue. "Julian, although your church and anchorhold in Carrow, Norwich, was destroyed by bombing during the Second World War, it's been rebuilt and is now not only a church but a study center, and your reconstructed anchorhold is a chapel where visitors can pray or reflect quietly; and there are images and sculptures of you at Norwich Cathedral, too. Hildegard, in Bingen, there are guidebooks and tourist walks that lead visitors to sites of importance during your lifetime. Francis, you and your town of Assisi attract huge numbers of tourists every year."

"I can vouch for your popularity, Francis. Assisi was attracting large numbers of pilgrims back in 1414 when I visited. And, remember, as a recognized holy woman, Julian was a visitation destination in the early fifteenth century, when it was my privilege to visit her," Margery reminisces. "Excuse the interruption, Annie. Please, go on."

"It's good to be reminded of the story of your meeting with Julian," I assure her. "And, you're a 'site' now too, Margery."

"I always was a sight," laughs Margery, and we all join in.

I refer to the notes again, "Your hometown of King's Lynn has guided walks for tourists and your story and the places associated with your life are prominent features of the walks. There's even a park bench dedicated to you."

"Well, I guess that just leaves you and me, Cloud," says Richard.

Cloud shrugs, not seeming to mind at all that I haven't mentioned him. Richard has a blank expression, and I can't tell if he's disappointed or resigned to being left off my list of 'travel sites.'

"Sorry, Cloud, but it's true," I smile. "As far as I know, you are not a pilgrim destination."

"Ah, but there are many people looking for me," Cloud chuckles.

"Haha," joins in Richard. "I've got no doubt that, if and when someone figures out who you are, there'll be busloads of travelers heading in your direction,"

Cloud shrugs again and gives a cheeky grin. "Richard, I think I'll adopt your earlier comment as my mantra: 'A mystery is not to be solved, but embraced.'"

"Now Richard, you're an interesting one," I announce, scanning my notes one last time before returning them to my pocket. "It's a fact that there aren't any actual buildings or sites associated with you that remain to attract tourists. Sad to say, even the shrine of your burial, and the priory associated with it, were dissolved sometime in the sixteenth century. Officially dissolved . . . but not forgotten. Archaeologists have been working in Hampole and at the priory site with a view to uncovering more information about you. So, who knows what the future might bring?"

Richard beams. "You know, for some years after my death, there were followers of my life and work who thought I might be a candidate for canonization. Apparently, miracles at my shrine were reported. But, as it turned out, God had other plans for me and I am delighted to hear that I'm still remembered and studied and, yes, even a bit of an archaeological site destination now. And that's not because of any pride or ego—I can say that with absolute honesty—but it's because, as you say, Annie, it means people today are interested in mystics. And if they're interested in mystics, they're probably in search of a clearer understanding of themselves.

"Well said, Richard," exclaims Francis springing to his feet from his spot on the floor. Pat is startled, and I see him watching for Francis's next move. When he realizes that Francis is just moving to the coffee table, he settles back down, adjusting his body this way and that in an effort to maximize the warmth on his back. "More coffee, tea, brandy anyone?" he asks, and then he makes his way to each of us, topping up our cups and glasses as required.

Richard accepts more coffee, takes a long sip, and puts the cup down on the table. I watch him stand up and reach into his coat pocket from which he produces a delicate box of light reddish-brown wood, smooth as satin. "Annie, please do the honors," he says, handing the box to me. Intrigued, I unclip the tiny iron clasp that's holding the box's lid to its base. I lift the lid to find inside is another box, smaller and of shiny white cardboard, tied with a gold ribbon. Opening this box reveals twelve exquisitely crafted chocolates. "Dolce," laughs Richard. "We've had the *canor*—the song from Francis; we've got the *calor*—the warmth of the fireside; here is the *dulcor*—the sweetness. The box was crafted from Yorkshire wild cherrywood many centuries ago by a hermit friend of mine. It's my gift of thanks to you. And don't worry, the chocolates aren't as aged. I purchased them earlier today from a chocolate shop in the city, and they're for us to share now."

"Thank you, Richard, it's really beautiful. I'll treasure it." I pass the box around and all the guests choose a chocolate.

"It's our turn now," Hildegard shouts, on her feet, her hands clapping us to attention. "We've promised Annie a summary of our insights, and some consideration of their modern applicability as appropriate, and we will do our best. However, I have to offer a word of caution at the outset. Mystics experience a deep, personal engagement with the Divine and thus it follows that, after such engagement, our lives are turned totally toward God. In that turning, though, if you're not a better person in your relationships with others, then you're not a true mystic."

"Not the 'real deal,'" I contribute.

"Precisely. 'Not the real deal' is a good way to describe those people who, even today, pretend to have their eyes fixed firmly on heaven when, in fact, they're more interested in looking at their bank account. But I digress." Hildegard draws herself up to her full height and continues with her caution, "Each person reading our texts will find different points of resonance and relevance too; things that help them in their relationship with God and with others. Our texts are what you might now call an 'immersive experience'; that is, readers enter more deeply into themselves and God as they progress, becoming changed in the process. As you will appreciate, then, it's no easy task to extract a point here and there and declare those points more relevant to one's life than other insights. That said, we have all tried to share our experiences for the benefit of everyone, and that's what we want to continue to do. Now, Annie," Hildegard says as she turns to me, "you're a modern woman, so it's appropriate that you do the one-line summaries of the key points as we discuss them."

"Oh, I doubt I could do that, Hildegard; certainly not with any justice to your insights," I reply, feeling quite nervous at the idea.

"We have confidence in you, Annie. Do your best," instructs Hildegard and, turning back to the group, she continues her address. "I've heard in various advertisements today, 'Any advice we give is general in nature and cannot substitute for consultation with a professional.' The 'professional' in our case is God. Perhaps that's the overarching and the underpinning insight for all mystical insights. God is our first and last referent. God is in everything we do; God is in us; and we have our life in God. Everything after that is elaboration on ways we can come to know God better. That's why God has given each mystic here a different experience of the Divine Presence. We have been enabled to offer a variety of perspectives on the one essential Truth. I'm sure, however, that we also have many points in common. So, please, I suggest, we deliver our points clearly but let us also allow for further discussion around those points, if we are so moved. Is that acceptable to everyone? Annie?"

"Yes, that sounds fine to me," I reply. "I don't want to trade our lovely dinner party conversation for a lecture."

"Quite right, Annie," says Hildegard with a sharp nod of her head. "If no one objects, I'll begin." Hildegard doesn't wait for objections to her proposal. "Good. So, you already have my first point: God is all things, all things are in God. Next point: Mystics see differently; they see the 'big picture.' In my visions, I was shown the entire sweep of human history, from the creation to the end of days. To us, that seems like an enormous amount of time and yet, compared to eternity, it's a pinprick." Hildegard pauses to take a sip of water.

"Seeing the 'big picture' is very important," says Julian. "You'll recall that I told you of seeing all creation in the palm of my hand. It was so tiny and insignificant compared to the immensity of the creator that I feared for its safety. But God assured me that it survived because it was greatly loved. When we see differently, we take a larger perspective on things. I was shown that all shall be well. That was a divine promise, but it may not mean that the promise is fulfilled in the way that we expect it to be, and perhaps, not even in our narrow lifetime. We have no choice but to persist, sometimes in darkness, but always in hope. That's the big picture."

"I understand what you're saying, Julian," Margery puts down her glass and takes up the conversation. "But, let's face it, it's hard to translate the big picture into everyday life, isn't it? Especially if one's day-to-day life is terrible; it's very hard to pin your hopes on a better future in the afterlife."

Julian brings her hands together in a prayer-like gesture. "Yes, Margery, you're so right. It's what we've been saying about mystical insights—they're about qualities and approaches that help us understand ourselves in relation to God, and to better live within that relationship. The insights give us a guide but it's we—everyday, ordinary people —who have to strive to translate them into practice. That's where faith comes in, I suppose. Life is never easy. It's full of challenges, heartaches, and unfathomable sadness, but it's also full of joy, excitement, and promise. That's the tension of life."

It's time to offer my brief summary, I realize. Swallowing my hesitation, I begin, "Today, we understand the 'big picture' as keeping things in perspective, or maybe taking a long-term view, though, as far as I know, we don't extend that view into the afterlife. We also think of it as not allowing ourselves to become bogged down in irrelevant details. We might say, 'Don't sweat the small stuff.'"

"I like that, Annie. You took a while to get to the one-liner but it's catchy." Hildegard looks pleased, and I don't bother to tell her that the phrase did not originate with me.

"Your summary is apt," agrees Julian. "We have to persist in the darkness of not knowing what might happen next to us, day-to-day, while at the same time, proceeding in the light of faith that promises an end to our woes and an eternity of bliss."

"It's a paradox, and it's a mystery," reflects Cloud. "Our life here is a tiny shadow on the expanse of eternity. It's very hard to get our heads around the big picture when our days are numbered. You know that I've talked about God making time for us to use? Well, perhaps if we put our attention in each moment—one, then the next, then the next—we can more easily accept the paradox, more effectively enter into the mystery."

"Should that be a point on our list, Cloud?" asks Francis, pretending to jot down something on the palm of his hand.

"Probably," agrees Cloud, "but I'll say more about it a bit later, so no need to take note of it yet, dear friend."

Francis pretends to wipe his palm clean with the other hand. We all laugh.

"What I can say now," continues Cloud, "in support of Hildegard's 'big-picture' is that, difficult as it seems to achieve, with prayer and practice it is possible to switch between the big awareness and tiny moment-to-moment awareness. It requires a change of habit (one of those things we talked about very early in the evening), of understanding that awareness of the infinite is present in the finite."

"The infinite, the eternal, breaks through into temporal life every now and then for all of us, not just mystics," emphasizes Hildegard.

"It's exactly as you say, Hildegard," says Richard. He goes on to explain. "We mystics have had extended glimpses of that divine reality. But most people get a glimpse, too, every now and then. Something out of the blue jolts them out of their sleep, and, for a moment, they see differently. For some, it's the huge shock of being diagnosed with a serious illness; for others, it's a small coincidence like bumping into an old friend just minutes after you'd thought of him for the first time in years."

"I think I know what you all mean," I say. "There are things in our lives, from positive occurrences like falling in love or unexpectedly getting your dream job to negative things like a marriage breakdown or the death of a dear friend, that shake us out of our everyday habits and make us think differently, do something differently. It's an intrusion of 'otherness' that reminds us that there's more happening, beyond the 'bandwidth' of our five senses."

"That's a good way to put it, Annie," says Cloud. "And the most amazing intrusion of otherness, as Hildegard has noted tonight, is the Incarnation. She explained that, in her visions, she saw that the coming of Jesus Christ split history apart. Sometimes I think of humans moving along the horizontal access of time, and I picture eternity as a vertical line; and when Christ came into history, the eternal bisected the horizontal. And you know what shape that makes? It makes a cross, the symbol of our faith."[2]

The conversation pauses here, as if, by unspoken mutual agreement, everyone has turned their thoughts to the symbol of the cross and the symbolism that Cloud has suggested.

Suddenly, Hildegard claps her hands again. "Perhaps it's time to move on to the next insight or two," she suggests. "Richard, what would you like to add?"

Richard interlocks his fingers and, turning his palms outward, stretches his arms in front of him. "Hmmm. Well, for me, a key insight is the importance of being aware, of paying attention to the movement of God in your soul. I've told you how this happened for me. It was when I made the decision to leave my studies. Although my family and friends did not understand why I had abandoned my master's degree, the stirrings of my soul could not be ignored. Later, when I received the fire of love and other divine apprehensions, I did not know how to respond at first. I had to sit with the feelings, quite literally; sit quietly, and give my total attention to what was occurring within me."

---

2. This elaboration of the idea of the symbol of the cross is a creative one. Although the author of *The Cloud of Unknowing* makes reference to the cross and its symbolic importance, in *The Book of Privy Counselling*, the idea of the Cross respresenting the bisecting of time with eternity was not, as far as the author knows, a medieval idea but, rather, one that gained prominence in the twentieth century with theologians such as Thomas Torrance. For further details, see Thomas F. Torrance, *Space, Time and Incarnation* (Oxford: Oxford University Press, 1969). See also Carmel Bendon Davis, *Mysticism and Space: Space and Spatiality in the Works of Richard Rolle, The Cloud of Unknowing Author, and Julian of Norwich* (Washington, DC: Catholic University of America Press, 2008), 132–34.

By now I'm feeling more at ease with the assignment Hildegard has set me, and so I say, "Although I understand that you are talking about a much stronger, deeper call to change your life, we might relate to that now more superficially as 'trusting your gut' or 'following your intuition.'"

Out of the corner of my eye, I see Hildegard giving the tiniest nod.

"Hmm... 'trusting your gut' is not a bad analogy, Annie," says Richard. "I certainly had to go deeply into myself to discern if I was about to take the right path. There, by being still and listening for God, I was able to take the action that I knew was God's will. I suppose what I'm talking about is the importance of prayer."

"Praying in that manner, by really going into our soul where God dwells, is very powerful," comments Francis. "The inward movement enables the outward movement of service for others. In my life, I spent as much time as possible in quiet, solitary places, simply being with God in my soul. And those times made it possible for me to travel and preach and assist those most in need. It is the same for all of us, I believe. The impetus, the energy, to write down for others the wonderful insights God gave us, is the natural outcome of tapping into the source of all energy and creativity within us, and that is God."

"We all understand the need for physical rest in order to recharge ourselves for our responsibilities, and prayer is the recharging method for our spiritual responsibilities," sums up Cloud.

"I'm thinking about your aligning of awareness, attention, and prayer," I say. "When I, along with Francis's help, brought the main course to the table, I was struck by the way that you, Cloud, suggested we all take a moment to look carefully at the meal before diving in to eat it. And you all looked, and you saw and appreciated colors and textures; and that encouraged me to look carefully, and to use my other senses, too, in the same way that you talked about re-enforcing memories by using all your senses; and just as you, Richard, told of the senses of your soul in experiencing God. When that main course arrived, all of you were totally in the moment, totally 'mindful' as we might say today, totally appreciating the food and the time and work spent in preparing it for you. And that encompassed gratitude, too, I presume."

"I was definitely very grateful for that food," laughs Richard. "And you're right, Annie. Being grateful, especially when that gratitude is given warmly to others and from there extends to God for all that we are given divinely, is a prayer in itself."

"And, interestingly, your highlighting of the careful attention we paid to your lovely meal brings together some of the previous points of relevance," exclaims Cloud. "As we've discussed, mystics see the 'big picture.' But to see the grander scale of things, you also have to be aware of the smaller things, the everyday things. And here I'm not talking about those irrelevant details that you mentioned a short while ago, Annie. I mean, if we are observant of what others are doing and saying and feeling, if we use all our senses in appreciation of what we've been given, and if we pause every now and then to appreciate, in silence, the hum of life around us, we will start to see differently, we will see the connection between things, we will begin to access some of the 'big picture,' which—as Julian shared with us in her beautiful image of creation being no bigger than the size of a hazelnut in comparison to the immensity of our uncreated creator—is God's view. Not literally God's view, of course, but when you're present to everyone and everything around you, then your soul—God's image in you—wakes up, as Richard has explained, and starts to feel and know God's presence, which brings us back to prayer."

"Ah, I get it. To see differently, you first have to look and become aware of the obvious," I announce, and then add my one-line contribution of, "Pay attention! Turn off auto-pilot."

"Precisely. Be awake to life in order to see beyond life. And once you do that . . ."

Margery stops Cloud's words by suddenly standing up and starting to pace around the room.

"Are you all right, Margery?" I ask with panic in my voice as my mind replays Margery's earlier falling episode.

"Yes, yes, perfectly fine. Please don't worry. It's just that I've had a little revelation of my own during this conversation. Cloud's lucid explanation of being still, and being observant, has made me realize that, in my lifetime, I was not still enough—hardly ever, in fact—to really notice those around me. I've long been aware that I'm a bit of a contentious inclusion on any list of medieval mystics. Oh, don't get me wrong, I don't doubt God's gifts to me, I don't doubt that I saw things differently, and I don't doubt that I accessed the bigger picture. But I do doubt that I looked carefully enough before doing so. I was a wife, a mother, a woman who had owned and worked in my own businesses; and then I became someone who was prepared to leave my husband and home and try to claim a religious life, when I had little or no hope of being professed. I'm honored to be part of this very wonderful company here, but I know, too,

Annie, that not everyone would be as welcoming of me as you and your truly beautiful guests have been."

"Then they would be the ones missing out," exclaims Richard.

"Very kind of you, Richard, but I know that then, and now, many viewed me as a fake, as someone who 'performed' as a mystic and holy woman for my own benefit—whatever they might have thought that to be. But, in my heart and soul, I *did* speak with God, continually. Yes, in retrospect, I can see that my external appearance and behavior were . . . a bit unusual. I might even agree that I wanted people to notice me. Perhaps that was my own vanity. But I truly wanted others to be aware of God's goodness, aware that if God could move someone like me to change my life, to give up my home and husband and social standing and stability, then God was real and available to everyone. Perhaps I leapt before I looked."

"You've given me something to think about, Margery," admits Cloud. "I painted a very negative picture of 'false contemplatives' in my writings, accusing them of manufacturing piety, based on my observations of their actions and behavior that, in many ways, they had in common with you. I didn't think about the idea that they may have wanted to draw attention to themselves for reasons other than personal gain. And, in our day . . ."

"Ah, but I don't disagree with you on that, dear Cloud." Margery is serious. She leans toward him. "You see, at some level, there *was* a need in me to be noticed. From the divine point of view, I know that God was working in my soul, not on how I looked to others. But I realize now that I could have been an example of holiness through quiet prayer and quiet kindness to others. Yet what was I to do about this strange gift of tears that I received?"

"Ha," laughs Hildegard, "perhaps, as they say, and I don't mean this unkindly, 'if you can't be a good example, you can be a terrible warning.' Not 'terrible' of course, but, I mean, you gave people something to really think about."

"Oh, Hildegard, that's one of the nicest things that anyone's ever said to me," smiles Margery as she walks over to Hildegard and embraces her.

"It's amusing, but it's also a worthy point that you make, Hildegard," reflects Julian. "I have lately read St. Teresa of Avila, and one of the many insightful observations she makes in her wonderful text, *Interior Castle*, is that we can all learn a lot from people who scandalize us.[3] When I first read that, it drew me up, challenged all my prejudices. But the more I thought about it, the more I knew it to be true. We can jump to conclusions about others based on their external appearance or behaviors. But we don't know their souls, their motivations, their pains; or, maybe even more pertinent, we don't know anything about their relationship with God. It is not our place to judge. Perhaps we are shocked by them because there is something in their behavior that we ourselves are guilty of in one form or another. We are all capable of becoming very comfortable with our perceived 'goodness,' our cozy self-righteousness, and yet, by looking at those whom we find shocking, we might learn something valuable about ourselves."

"Coming up against people with stridently held opinions that are vastly different from our own can bring out our

---

3. See Teresa of Avila, *Interior Castle*, trans. and ed. E. Allison Peers, (Mineola, NY: Dover Publications, 2007), 45.

angry opposition, but those same people are also helping us to know ourselves and to define our opinions and values more clearly," comments Cloud. "In a way, they are holding a mirror to us and, sometimes we will see our prejudices reflected back. Of course, we must stand up for what is right, but perhaps we should weigh the words, not judge the speaker, just as we should judge the deed but not the doer."

"Yes, so being non-judgmental is definitely on the relevance list," I confirm.

"Oh, I'm so sorry," cries Margery. "You see, there I go again, taking the attention to me and my issues when we were in the middle of helping Annie with the relevance list."

"Actually, Margery, I think you've helped the process," says Francis. "We've now added the importance of leaving judgment to God. I remember that you, Julian, received insight into two sorts of judgement—one earthly, one divine. And right here, Cloud has set out how this works in practice: on earth, it is right and necessary to judge the wrong-doing that offends and causes pain to others, and then to apply justice to the deed, while leaving the final judgment of the doer to God."

"Well, as I know I've sometimes offended, perhaps then I should add some of my own insights here, based on my life and experience," suggests Margery. She looks around and, as we are all nodding in agreement, she goes on. "As you know, in my life, many people were against me and tried to discredit me. As a consequence, I spent a lot of time and energy seeking validation until I realized that, in the unpredictable messiness of life, only God is unchanging. In short, God is the steady, still point in the midst of all the chaos and, if we focus on that still point, then we are safe, regardless of whatever happens."

"And, in short, we might say today, 'Keep your eyes on the prize' and 'Stay calm.' Don't get drawn into others' dramas."

"Very sensible, Annie. And, again thanks to Margery's example, I think you could add the importance of honesty to your list," Francis says. "Margery, you held nothing back in showing your devotion to God. I know you downplay your contribution to the people of your own time and beyond, but be assured, your pilgrimages and the overt signs of your God-given gifts were a true sign to society. And perhaps, even if you are correct that you were not still enough, often enough, you surely inspired others to reflect on what you were about and on what they themselves were about. As Cloud might say, you were a mirror to your society, and interest in your life today might have the same effect."

It looks like Margery is wiping away a tear as she responds, "Francis, that is very, very kind of you. Every one of you here is so kind. I will reflect on what you have all said to me."

"And your level of honesty indicates a high degree of self-knowledge, which makes it the perfect time to hear Cloud's insights," announces Richard.

Cloud makes one of his little bows and obliges. "I'm a straightforward man. I shall be brief in my summation. My first insight, as I've said several times in the course of the evening, is that God cannot be reached by thought but only by love. My second is that, to truly reach out with love, we need humility, which is nothing more than the real knowledge of ourselves in relation to our creator. And when we really come to know ourselves as we are, we come to know God. My third insight is that God has made time for us, and it benefits us to make use of every moment as an opportunity to move closer to God; heaven can be won or lost in the blink of an eye. Finally, a good will, a good intent, directed toward God is what God sees; not our failings."

"Succinct as you've been, Cloud, there's a lot in what you've said," observes Hildegard. "Could you say a little more about the time issue?"

"Certainly," agrees Cloud. "God has made time for us, but we also have free will. This means that in any and every moment, there are decisions and choices we can make. Too many waste their time on empty pursuits. Of course, there is nothing wrong with leisure, a holiday, a good sleep when it's needed. And there's something wonderful about being with friends and sharing good food and conversation, as we're doing this evening. These things are not wasting time. The empty pursuit is one that does not move us forward in love for God, or for others, or for ourselves. And we've spoken about the paradox of our lives being passed in time but having their ultimate existence in eternity. Thus, for the benefit of our souls, we need to consider making choices that take eternity into account."

"And that means being awake and aware of the big picture," says Richard, bringing several points of the conversation together.

"Today, we might say, 'Life is short; you never know how long you've got, so make it count,'" I comment. "However, the trouble with today is that we live at a frantic pace, and we never seem to have time to sit quietly and reflect on the very thing you're talking about, Cloud. We are so overloaded with information—and it's available in the palm of our hand via our phones. We are easily distracted because we are spoiled with choices, you might say. We see so many options that might be relevant to our search and so we chase them, first this one, then that, but we're not looking in the right place."

"Humans have always been easily distracted, Annie," Cloud assures me. "'The spirit indeed is willing, but the flesh is weak' (Matt 26:41). It is, as I've said, about putting our attention in each moment, then the next, and the next. A moment of true awareness can stretch quite a way."

"I'm going to try to keep that thought in mind next time I'm tempted to play idly with my phone," I declare. "And, Cloud, since you're elaborating on certain points, I'd really like to hear more on humility. You explained it as being true self-knowledge, seeing ourselves as we really are, with our faults and failings, coupled with the realization that, despite our lowliness, God loves us unreservedly. This makes humility so positive and powerful—a way to be better, kinder to others in our everyday dealings—but I don't think we see it as a good quality today. Instead, we are bombarded with images and messages of high-profile, successful, and wealthy people, who are famous for being famous. And the name of the game is self-promotion: see this, wear that, eat here, travel there. It's true that ordinary people can feel quite intimidated, quite dissatisfied with their own unglamorous lives. In fact, I think, some feel downright miserable because they are measuring themselves against the false images that constantly fill our screens."

Hildegard's voice cuts through the room. "You're astute in calling them 'false images.' First commandment: 'You shall have no gods before me.'"

Stroking Pat's back, Francis says reflectively, "Humility has always been in very short supply, especially among the rich, the famous, and the powerful. Many of those influential individuals or groups really do see poorer people as inferior. And that gives a boost to the false image they have of themselves."

"It's the complete opposite of humility—getting a boost in your self-perception by seeing others as inferior, rather than getting a demotion in your self-perception by being aware of your smallness in comparison to the immeasurable greatness of God," explains Richard.

"And that's humility—knowing that there is something far, far greater than us, knowing that we are created yet loved unconditionally by our creator," Cloud adds.

I'm nodding. "These are very challenging ideas for us today. I've already shared my opinion that humility comes a poor second to self-esteem these days. From my observation, what we call self-esteem seems often to be akin to an inflated ego and a generous portion of self-congratulations; seeing the good parts of ourselves and ignoring those aspects that could do with some improvement. I know I'm guilty of that."

"You might be right, Annie, and I know you're speaking from your heart, in honesty. But self-knowledge is also about balance," explains Hildegard.

I notice Cloud knitting his brows before he speaks. "That's right, Hildegard. It's important to recognize your failings but then not beat yourself up too much about them. Accept them, be sincerely sorry for them, try to rectify them, and then open your heart and love more."

"Hmmm. Sound advice, Cloud." Hildegard is holding the liqueur glass out, swirling the remaining brandy around. She puts the glass to her lips and swallows the contents in one quaff. She begins speaking, a little hesitantly, "In the light of honest reflection, as has been our manner tonight, I have to admit that there were times when my pride led me to feel overconfident in my abilities when, in reality, deep down, I knew that it was God working through me. Equally, however, I confess that every now and then, doubts about my abilities would beset me, and I would question myself and wonder why God had chosen a weak, uneducated woman like me, when there were many, more powerful and well-educated men around. And that, dear friends, was questioning God's wisdom; not mine. Thus, that was my pride again, in another form. I learned, slowly but surely, to trust God and to align myself wholeheartedly with God's will. There is no other way."

"Our self-doubts are a scourge, aren't they?" I say in agreement with Hildegard's honest summation. "Today, in the interests of our psychological health, we are warned to be vigilant against negative self-talk, and you are advising the same thing, albeit for a slightly better, more spiritual reason. My short version of this is easy: Be kind to yourself, for you are only human."

"Exactly. It's important that we are not the ones holding ourselves back by thinking negatively about our proven abilities. We need to be brave in stepping into our roles, whatever they are," stresses Hildegard. "Francis, perhaps you can say something about this, and give us your recommendations for the list, too."

Francis, now semi-reclining on the floor near the fire, laughs loudly. "My first lesson: keep it simple. And actually, it's all simple, isn't it, in theory. Live simply, take no more than you need, and share anything that you have in abundance—material or spiritual. Love God, love others, rejoice in God's creation, and take care of it. I would only add—and Richard has touched on it, and all of you know it and have lived it—

that, while the meaning of our life here is to come to know ourselves in order to love God, the purpose is to be of service."

"Thank you, Francis. I think you've just done the summary for me." I breathe a sigh of relief.

"You certainly lived your lesson, Francis, in your simple life of poverty and service," says Julian, "but you also accomplished great things. As Annie has told us, you are venerated to this very day for your service to the poor, and for your love and care of all God's creatures."

"And for the vital and continuing gift of focusing our awareness on the care for our planet today," I hasten to add. "That is, as we've discussed, God working through you, Francis, and others, over time, reminding us, in this case, to respect all creatures.

"God required it of me. Sometimes in life, something courageous is required of us all. It might not be as drastic as stripping naked in the town piazza and renouncing your old life, or going to the pope to demand that the Church be rebuilt, but there will be times in each person's life when it is necessary to speak out for those who cannot—for your child, for the poor, the homeless, the refugee, and the suffering animal. Service to others is the fulfillment of God's call to us and the following of Jesus's example."

"It's the necessary outcome of mystical awakening," Richard joins in. "As we've so often said, our insights were never for ourselves alone. We were privileged to see differently and that carried with it a responsibility to do differently, and to share our visions."

"Yes, to spread hope, especially to those who might feel hopeless," says Julian.

"I understand what you're all saying: seeing differently calls you to live differently. And I've got to agree, you're all shining examples of taking on the responsibility," I say. "Francis, you traded a life of wealth and prestige for poverty and simplicity, and you persisted in winning a pope over to approve your radical new order of begging friars. Hildegard, your cosmic visions and your interpretation of them, and the production of your other works in music, drama, and natural science are extraordinary, even when compared to today's high-tech outputs. And Julian, the courageous articulation of your revelations of hope and love in a time of pestilence and social upheaval, and all from the confines of a tiny anchorhold out into the wide world, is amazing. Cloud and Richard, you both turned your backs on material comfort and worldly prestige to take up a life of solitude and prayer. Margery, when God called you, you answered unreservedly and quite literally put yourself on display as a living example of some-one fired with God's love as you traversed much of the known world. So, you really had the courage of your convic-tions; as we say, you 'walked the talk.' Oh dear, I feel I'm not expressing this very well." I pause and look around at my guests.

Cloud sighs. "Don't be too hard on yourself, Annie. We, your guests, have had a lifetime under God's loving guidance to learn the deepest lessons of the soul. However, what you're saying about 'walking the talk' is worthwhile. God en-abled us to 'see' better and, having been given that privilege, it was necessary to follow through, or to live a lie for the rest of our lives. That is, if you've seen more, you should pray for the courage to do more, to live your life in harmony with your soul. The follow-through doesn't have to be earth-shat-tering, just the sharing of whatever gifts God has given. Serv-ice to others can take many forms."

"That's right," agrees Francis. "Not everyone can go wandering out into the world, feeding the poor or starting hospitals. Not everyone can retire to a cave in the mountains and spend their life in prayer; not everyone can—nor should they—put their life aside for a grand ideal. The world needs many kinds of vocations, many kinds of workers and lifestyles. But whatever the life, everyone can act morally and justly with those in their family and in their community. Everyone can be kind."

Julian inclines her head, and the movement is enough to draw our attention to her before she quietly observes, "We have discussed the importance of prayer in our own spiritual lives but prayer is also a great service that we can do for others."

"Probably the most powerful service of all," agrees Francis. "Everyone needs prayer; everyone benefits from prayer—the one praying, and the one being prayed for. And Julian, you've been listening attentively to all our recommendations for today. Please share yours with us."

"Gladly," smiles Julian. "I had requested more time to get my thoughts together and you have all been very gracious in giving me the broad sweep of your wonderful insights. Of course, all that you have shared is in line with all that God revealed to me. As we've said, while the divine truths are unchanging, each of us has received a different slant on them, which makes it all the better for readers today. A choice of perspectives, let's say, but, like light refracted through a prism, there is only one light source." Julian takes a breath before saying, "There are three points I'd like to highlight. First, I'd recommend reflection, as it is both a form of prayer and an important use of time, and certainly an essential tool for self-knowledge. As I've told you, I wrote two versions of my revelations. I've explained that the first was an account of the immediate experience, which was wonderful and astounding; the second, an expanded version, was the outcome of many years of reflection. Often, and this was the case with me, we are too amazed or shocked by certain happenings to comprehend fully their complete significance at first. But our brains and hearts still store them, and our faith preserves them, and by reflecting on them with God's guidance, we learn to understand their significance, and our lives in God, more deeply. Reflection is a journey into self-knowledge and, therefore, into God."

"Reflection on the good and the bad in our life gives us a valuable perspective on the workings of God in time," Hildegard points out.

"Quite so, Hildegard," Julian says. "And, in some ways, this is related to my next point, which is about hope in God. As you know, I was shown that all shall be well, and this is an assurance that we can rightly expect to continue in eternal happiness after our earthly life in eternal happiness. We need not fear, we need never despair, as long as our will is fixed in hope. Even if we are overtaken by dreadful illness or other suffering, I was shown that, at death, God takes us from woe to bliss in the blink of an eye. Before the coming of miracles, there is always a time of sorrow and anguish."

"Julian, hope is such a marvelous virtue," says Cloud. "Your words resonate with our discussion on the importance of the way we see life. It's not just about the here and now, but about being open to a larger view that takes in wonderful possibilities and acknowledges that God is a certainty in which we can trust. God is the certainty within the uncertainty. And, as life in this world is so uncertain, why put all our trust and energy into what is transient? Why not consider transcendence?" Cloud laughs, making a generous circular sweep of his arm to indicate more expansive possibilities.

"Why not, indeed?" agrees Julian. "And, Cloud, your mention of trust is crucial. For God's love to flow through us, we have to surrender control—well, really, our illusion that we're in control. This brings me to my third point: even though we are assured of eventually being taken from our pain and suffering, our human nature makes us ponder why God allows suffering. We may not like the reason, but I was shown that troubles make us cry out for God's help: we pray and we are heard; we are reminded of our fragility, and yet also of how greatly God loves us. God will always answer, but not always in the manner that we expect. And suffering is the other side of love. Jesus suffered for us because his love for us was so immense. As I was shown, seeing the loved one suffer is more painful than suffering ourselves. We learn a great deal from this paradox. Through the ordinariness of everyday suffering, we see the extraordinariness of love." Julian leans back in her chair and closes her eyes.

"Seeing the extraordinary through the ordinary," Margery echoes. "It's like seeing the hand of God in every part of creation, as Hildegard and Francis have already shared . . . the universe, the planet, the oceans, the mountains, every leaf, every unique fingerprint. . . . Back to being aware, too!"

"Julian, you've given me so many important things to add to my list, I'm not sure if I can summarize them in one line," I confess.

"Let's call it, 'staying positive,'" suggests Cloud with a smile.

We all smile with him, but Julian really has given us so much to consider that a quiet pause comes over the room. I let it linger for a minute or two before saying, "Thank you all so much for helping me sum up a tiny portion of all that you have experienced in your mystical life. I know that the breadth and depth of your insights cannot be conveyed in single phrases or catchy lines. I know, too, however, that people are searching for God, for meaning, and you have much to offer those who seek you out and engage more thoroughly with you. As you've made clear, God is beyond words, your mystical experiences are beyond words, and yet you have been generous enough to communicate something of the essence of what you have received. And, for that, I thank you with all my heart."

"Don't thank us too soon," warns Hildegard. "We've left the most important qualities to the last. These are the golden threads through the fabric of our mystical insights, and we all hold these threads in common. Who would care to do the honors?" Hildegard casts her eyes around the room.

"I'll begin," agrees Richard.

By this stage, I am not surprised that all their thoughts are in synchronicity. They've been reading my thoughts all evening!

"*Wonder*," announces Richard. "Amid all the turmoil, every age has its wonderful aspects. Your world today is full of marvelous things, of incredible inventions and advances. Technology is a wonder; the way in which you can fly to the other side of the world in less than a day, or find information at the press of a few buttons, or talk to your loved ones on the other side of the world via a screen—see their faces, hear their voices—are all wonders. Science is a wonder; modern medicine is a wonder. These are wonders that the medieval world could not have imagined. You are surrounded, inundated, by wonders, but amid the noise and haste of these wonders it becomes harder and harder to hear the voice of God and to appreciate the brilliance of God's creation. Do not overlook the beauty in the changing seasons, the brightness and immensity of the night sky, the delicate perfection of the newborn baby. Take time to wonder."

"*Mystery*," announces Cloud. "We are human. Our rational minds are limited. There is so much we cannot know. God is Mystery. We are in God. We are enclosed in Mystery. Be sure to enjoy the privilege."

"*Love*," announces Julian. "God is Love. And Love is the image of God in each and every soul. That's all we need to remember."

And, spontaneously, we each bow our heads, and in my heart I think of Julian's summation in her revelations of divine love. And suddenly I know that all the guests, and even Pat, are thinking and praying the same prayer, inspired by God's words to Julian:

Many times, I have wondered what the deepest meaning of my life is. And God has answered me thus: Know it well. Love is the meaning.[4]

---

4. See Julian of Norwich, *Showings* (Long Text), ed. Edmund Colledge and James Walsh. Classics of Western Spirituality Series (New York: Paulist Press, 1978), 342.

Farewell

It is time for the guests to leave. One minute we are sitting, finishing the last of our brandy, and the next I hear the old grandfather clock in the hallway strike the hour.

"Midnight," cries Hildegard. "Well, Annie, it's time we departed." And just like that, she stands from the chair and is gathering up her black satchel. She is ready to go. The others follow her lead, standing up, putting cups and glasses neatly back on the tray on the coffee table, no doubt to save me too much effort afterwards.

I feel bereft. "You don't have to leave yet, you know," I assure them, and can hear the note of pleading in my voice. "We can put more logs on the fire, and I can make some fresh coffee...or maybe some hot chocolate...or chamomile tea, if you're worried about getting to sleep after too much caffeine."

They seem not to hear me. They are happy, still chatting to each other as they bustle down the hallway toward the front door. I follow until we're all gathered in a tight little group in the entrance hall.

"Annie, dear," says Julian, turning to put a gentle arm around my waist, "your hospitality has been exceptional. The food, the warmth, the care, the company, and the wonderful conversation have lifted my heart. But we cannot stay forever. Nobody can. When it is time to go, we must go promptly, without dawdling, without regret, for what lies ahead will be greater than what we leave behind, even when what we are leaving has been as extraordinary and special as our evening with you tonight." She lets me go and, with head held high, steps to the coat stand to retrieve her coat, which she puts on effortlessly, and takes up her folded umbrella from the stand's base. Then she walks to the door and stands motionless, looking outward, ready to go.

"But you can visit us in your prayers, your meditations, and, of course, there are always the tourist and archaeological possibilities," Richard says with a smile. "Thank you most sincerely, Annie. It has been an evening to remember always." He takes my hand, lifts it to his lips, and brushes a light kiss across the back of it. Then he heads to the coat stand, takes down his elegant topcoat, wraps it around his shoulders in one smooth arc, and moves to the front door, too.

Margery, who had been struggling to put her ankle boots back on, has now managed the task and is buttoning up her coat. "It's been wonderful, Annie. The best evening of the century, so far. Here," she says, as she reaches into her coat pocket, pulls out a little package wrapped in rough fabric, and places it in my hand, "a small thank you gift from me. From my heart. Open it later." And she leans in and embraces me, planting a kiss first on one check, then the other. She steps back and, from the other pocket, takes out her mobile phone. "Please excuse me. I'm just ordering an Uber ride home for Julian and me. Can I offer anyone a ride with us?" She sweeps her gaze around the circle of friends in the hallway.

"Francis, maybe you need a ride," I suggest.

"Aw, no thanks. I always walk when I can. And when I can't, someone usually gives me a ride, or there's always public transport." Francis is on the floor again, this time putting his no doubt still-damp sneakers back on.

"Francis, you didn't arrive with a coat. I'm sure I have a spare somewhere that you can have. Or another sweater, or at least an umbrella," I offer.

"No, thank you. No need. I'm always well protected, in any weather," he grins as he jumps to his feet. "Thanks for everything, Annie. It's meant a lot to me," he whispers.

"What next for you, Francis?" I ask as I reach to take his hand in farewell. In response, he wraps me into a warm embrace and then, stepping back, he smiles at me and answers, "That, my dear friend, is entirely up to the will of God. And to wherever Brother Wind propels me next. Perhaps I will find myself on the streets on Kolkata, assisting the nuns in the service of the poor; or perhaps I will be in South America helping with disaster relief after an earthquake; or bandaging the limbs of koalas burnt in bushfires in Australia. Perhaps I will be sitting on a bench in a park in a big city in the United States, sharing a sandwich and chatting with a homeless person. For someone like me, there is never a shortage of demand and possibility."

He turns and walks away, and before I even have time to think about it, he is out the door and gone, into the night.

"No ride for me, either," calls Hildegard, now cloaked and ready to go. "I travel very well alone." She gives no hint as to the mode of her travel.

"I'm much the same," calls Richard from his position near the door. "I make my own way, in my own way, if you know what I mean."

And the other guest, the mysterious Cloud, is nowhere in sight.

"I think he went back to collect something in the dining room," offers Margery, seeing me glancing around. "Don't worry. With Cloud, there is no need for a formal farewell. We shall all see each other if and when it is needed."

A car horn sounds, and the Uber is here. How unbelievably prompt! We all step outside onto the porch together. The rain has stopped, the clouds are dispersing and, overhead, a bright full moon shines down on us.

Hildegard opens her satchel again. "This is for you, Annie. A little remembrance of our evening," she says. And there, in my hand, is an intricate image—hand-drawn and vividly colored—in the very style of Hildegard's own representations of her visions. As my eyes adjust to the moonlight, I see that it is an image of the cosmic egg. It is beautiful, mesmerizing. Nevertheless, I look up from it to wave a farewell to Hildegard, but in the moment I have been glancing at her gift, she has gone.

And so have Margery and Julian and Richard. Just like Francis, they have evaporated into the night, leaving no trace. I know that Cloud has gone, too, departing as quietly and mysteriously as he arrived.

I stand quite still and inhale the silence of the night. Everything smells fresh after the rain. The moonlight reflects on perfect drops of water dotting the leaves of the gardenias that surround the porch. The drops shimmer like . . . emeralds. I can feel how alive my front garden is after the downpour, pulsing with the *viriditas* of being. I take one more deep breath—in and out—and think about the inevitability of arrivals and departures in life; of the rollercoaster of happiness and the sadness; of the intimate dance of love and pain. After one last look over the quiet midnight garden, I walk back into my house, closing the front door firmly behind me.

I make my way slowly into the dining room to put out the candles but, suddenly, I feel very tired and take a seat at the table. I look around at each empty chair, picturing Hildegard here, Richard there, and so on. When my gaze lands on the seat Margery occupied, I remember the small package she had thrust into my hands as she left. I'd placed it in my skirt pocket and now take it out and examine it. The wrapping is some kind of undyed, broadly woven material, coarse and wonderfully textured, and I guess that it is probably made from flax. As I lay the little parcel on the table in front of me, I imagine Margery finding this piece of cloth somewhere in her cottage and repurposing it for my gift. The flaxen covering is tied with string which undoes easily with one pull, and it falls open to reveal an almost flat object, about the size of a large coin but cream or beige in its uneven coloring. I adjust my glasses and take a more concentrated look. It's a brooch, or a badge. . . . Ah, it's a scallop shell set in a delicate metal border; the metal is tarnished, but I suspect that it's bronze. I pick it up and turn it over to discover that the catch plate with its pin and clasp on its reverse side are still perfectly intact. "Oh Margery," I sigh, "it is your Santiago de Compostela pilgrim badge." When I opened the parcel, I'd noticed a small piece of folded parchment underneath the badge and I reach for it now. It's a note, the penmanship awkward but clear,[1] and it reads:

---

1. Margery's reading and writing skills were very limited. Even the composition of her book was only achieved when, after much searching, Margery found someone who was prepared to write her story as she dictated it.

To Annie, a fellow pilgrim. For the journey. Wherever it takes you, know that my prayers go with you. Margery Kempe.

I scoop up Margery's note and gift, wrapping and all, and put them back in my pocket to examine more carefully later. What a blessed evening it has been, I think, as I stand up and walk around the table, extinguishing the almost burnt out candles as I go. Something at the base of the last candlestick catches my eye. I stare and see another tiny package, this one simply wrapped in white paper, encircled with a silvery ribbon and, attached to the ribbon, a plain white card on which is clearly printed: "To Annie, with eternal thanks." I know Cloud has left it there for me to find. It's all too much. I blow out the candle, pick up the parcel, and pop it into my pocket with Margery's gift, having decided to unwrap it when I sit by the fire later, as soon as the cleaning up is done.

Back in the kitchen, Pat is looking at me with sad eyes. He lies on his bed in the corner and watches me loading the dishwasher. He's still keeping me in his sights as I stand at the sink, scrubbing the pot that held the risotto my guests liked so much. As I scrub, my mind replays their generous enthusiasm for the meal, the honesty and warmth of their conversation, and their thoughtful (and unexpected) gifts. I complete the pot cleaning and wipe the countertops. Then I make some peppermint tea. From the kitchen dresser, I take Julian's gifts which she had given me on her arrival—a book of her showings and the violets from her anchorhold garden—and put them on the tray with the tea and my cup, and head to the living room and the warmth of the fire.

"Okay, Pat. Come on. I could use the company," I say as the dog scrambles to his feet in expectation of . . . what? Does he think Francis might still be about? No, Pat is an animal of exquisite intuition; a dog who never misses an opportunity for food, or fun, or friendship. He knows Francis and the others have departed, and I can tell by the confident tread of his paws that he's now going to resume his responsibilities of diligently looking out for me.

I put the tray down on the coffee table before topping up the fire with a log. It ignites instantly, bright sparks flying in every direction. Ah, the fire of love, I think. I unload the tray, making the vase of Julian's violets the centerpiece. Then I unpack the contents of my pocket onto the table, placing the items in easy reach of the armchair I'm heading for. Before I sit, I pour a cup of tea. My attention is drawn to Hildegard's brown bottle of medieval brandy on the side of the table and, as if inviting me to have a nightcap, there's also a clean, unused liqueur glass right next to it. I get the hint, Hildegard, I laugh, and pour a small amount for myself. I settle back comfortably, as Pat positions himself between me and the fire. Set out on the low table in front of me are all the gifts from my guests. Next to Hildegard's exquisite brandy is the equally exquisite carved cherrywood box from Richard. I stretch for it and am amused to find, on lifting the lid, that one perfect dark chocolate treat remains. I don't have to think twice before popping it into my mouth. Recalling Richard's spiritual perceptions, I savor the rare sweetness of this chocolate; and I already have *calor* in the fire's warmth. All I need is the *canor*. Oh, how could I have forgotten? I spring from the chair and stride back to the kitchen. Where is it? I lurch back and forth, looking, looking until, at last, I see it on the windowsill. My phone.

"No stress, Pat," I call ahead as I hurry back to the living room, only to find as I reach it that Pat is not only completely unconcerned by my frantic search but that he is sound asleep and snoring. "Pat, I thought you'd be interested to know that I was looking for my phone so that I could play you Francis singing his 'Canticle of Dinner.'" Pat remains in dreamland, but I sit back and listen to the beautiful voice and the heartfelt words. What a gift! I close my eyes and send a silent prayer of thanks to Francis, wherever he might be heading.

And now I reach forward to take a closer look at the other gifts, one at a time. I first pick up Margery's pilgrim shell badge. It's light in my hand but I almost sense something of the gravity of emotions—the pains and joys of the journey—of its original wearer. Richard's cherrywood box is next to me on the arm of the chair, and so I place Margery's badge into it; it's the perfect place for it. Next, there is Hildegard's image of her cosmic egg. It's small, about the same size as a representation of an actual egg would be if drawn in two dimensions. It's on a piece of very fine vellum[2] and the colors are vibrant. I've read a little about the making of colored inks in the Middle Ages and, as I take in the beauty of the image, I'm fairly sure that the rich blue here is ultramarine[3] and that the gold stars are of actual gold leaf. This gift is precious in every way, and I'm pleased that it, too, fits comfortably in the cherrywood box for safekeeping. Julian's gift

---

2. Vellum and parchment are writing surfaces that were widely used in Western Europe, prior to the introduction of paper. Both surfaces are prepared from animal skins, but vellum, from calfskin, was usually of higher quality than other parchments, which were made from a variety of animal skins.

3. The rarest and most expensive color of the Middle Ages was *blue*, made from ultramarine, a powdered form of the semi-precious stone lapis lazuli and at that time sourced only from Afghanistan.

of the handwritten book of showings is also precious and, as I run my hands over the leather on the boards that constitute the book's covers, I marvel at the ingenuity of medieval bookbinding. When I open the book, I have even more to marvel at: the rough-cut parchment pages with their even handwriting in dark brown ink and the words not only written but experienced by Julian herself, in her magnificent visions, and transcribed here for me.

I can barely comprehend the generosity of all these gifts—not in the material sense but in the thought, the time, and the effort that my guests have given to them. I'm overcome with emotion. And it's then, out of the corner of my eye, that I catch sight of Cloud's gift, with its white paper and silver ribbon. It's peeping out from behind Hildegard's brandy bottle. I realize I must have obscured it when I put the bottle back after pouring my nightcap. I take it up carefully, and re-read the card's short message: "To Annie, with eternal thanks." I untie the ribbon and fold back the paper. Lying there is a small handle-less mirror, circular, simply set in a thin, carved frame of dark wood and backed by the same kind of wood. I pick it up carefully and look into it. I see myself reflected back and, yet, not myself. Something about the familiar face looks different. Or is it just that I am beginning to see differently?

Perhaps that's another remarkable gift of the mystics who came to dinner.

Glossary

Anchorhold. The dwelling of an anchorite or anchoress. In medieval Britain and Western Europe, the anchorhold was usually a small cell attached to the side of a church. In form, the anchorhold featured an entrance door—locked from the outside—and two or three windows: one, often called the "squint," that opened into the church and through which the anchorhold's occupant could receive the Eucharist; the second opening to an ante-room or the outside and through which the occupant received food and drink; a third (if included) opening into the public space.

Anchoress/anchorite (from Gk. *anachoresis*—"without company"). A woman ("anchoress") or man ("anchorite") who willingly was enclosed (immured) for life in a small cell ("anchorhold") in order to pursue a solitary life of prayer and contemplation. Such individuals were a particular feature of religious dedication and practice in medieval England. Anchoresses and anchorites were under the supervision of the local bishop and subject to rules of the Church and a nominated spiritual director. Those seeking enclosure usually required funds of their own and/or sponsorship to embark on the life but subsequently were wholly or partially maintained by people of the town or parish. From the thirteenth to sixteenth centuries, enclosure of females outnumbered those of males four to one.

Athomus. In medieval reckoning, the smallest unit of time; a time expression used to indicate the notion of something happening instantaneously or immediately, "in the blink of an eye." Although now officially considered to be fifteen ninety-fourths of a second, current estimates of the medieval opinion on the size of an athomus in relation to time is that there were about twenty thousand of them in an hour; therefore, each athomus was equal to one-sixth of a second.

Hagiography. Written account of a holy person's life. Unlike a biography, the hagiography emphasizes the holy and spiritual aspects of the subject's life rather than factual details.

Hermit. An individual who retired from mainstream life in order to live a solitary life devoted to prayer. Unlike medieval anchorites and anchoresses, who were of fixed abode in a town or village and dependent on others for support, hermits made their home in any number of available dwelling places, such as in caves, abandoned cottages, or geographically isolated places. They were entirely self-sufficient, self-directed, and self-supporting, often maintaining themselves by providing a community service such as offering refreshment for travelers, or assisting them across a stream, in exchange for small amounts of money or provisions. By the later Middle Ages, female hermits were frowned upon in England, because the commonly held view was that women could not be self-directing or self-supporting but, instead, should always be under male supervision if they wanted to pursue a solitary life.

Humility *topos*. A *topos* is a term used in literature to refer to a traditional theme or subject. The humility *topos*—downplaying learning or skill—was adopted frequently by medieval women who sought to put forward their own ideas, as women were prohibited from publicly speaking or writing without the approval of the Church or other recognized male authority.

Legenda. A book or collection of lessons prepared after a holy person's death in the expectation that this person's holiness in life would be recognized and that canonization would follow. The *legenda* often formed part of the daily prayers of those petitioning for the canonization.

Manuschristi. A concoction of crushed pearls, gold, rosewater, chopped lemon, spices, marzipan, and sugar, prepared especially by the Dominican monks of Bologna as a healing medicine for patients with a range of illnesses and medical conditions. It was believed to be so effective that it was given the name "the hand of Christ."

Medieval. Originally a word derived from the Latin *medium aevum* meaning "Middle Age." Fifteenth-century humanists had introduced the phrase "Middle Ages" to refer, in retrospect, to the historical period between the Classical and Modern eras. In the nineteenth century, *medium aevum* was contracted to "medieval" and used as a general term to refer to that (almost) thousand-year stretch of history between the sack of Rome by the Visigoths in 410 CE until about 1500 CE.

Mendicant. A member of a religious order (such as the Franciscans) who preached and prayed in various places, and who, having no personal or community possessions or property, begged for food and support along the way.

Minorite. A Franciscan friar, a member of the Franciscan order/brotherhood.

Mystic. One who has had a direct experience of God and endeavors to share that experience with others for their benefit.

Mysticism. An experiential, subjective, and personal apprehension of the Divine; a feature of all the world's great religious traditions.

Mystical theology. A branch of theology that is based on experiential rather than intellectual knowledge of God; the exact (Christian) origin is uncertain, but it was expounded at least as early as the time of Clement of Alexandria (c.150–215 CE).

Neuma. An early form of musical notation, used before the invention of modern five-line staff notation. Neuma used inflected marks above words to be sung, the marks indicating the general shape and direction (higher or lower) the sounds should take.

Neurotheology. A relatively new branch of science that studies the links between the human brain and spirituality, religious belief, and religious practice.

Plainchant. Unaccompanied liturgical singing or chanting of words in a regular pattern over a whole line or verse.

Pseudo-Dionysius. A Syrian monk of the early fifth century whose work on mystical theology and the *via negativa* was translated into (Middle) English by the Cloud author under the title, *Dionise Hid Divinite* ("Dionysius's Mystical Teaching").

Parchment. Prepared animal skin used as a writing surface in medieval times throughout Western Europe prior to the introduction of paper.

Quadrivium. Upper division of the "seven liberal arts" that were considered essential for the development of the thinking skills that denoted a well-educated person in the classical and medieval periods; the "Quadrivium" consisted of the study of four subjects: arithmetic, geometry, music, and astronomy.

Scintillating scotoma. Colored spots and points of light that flicker in front of, and often obscure, the visual field; may be experienced before the onset of a migraine headache.

Scribe. One who writes or copies documents or manuscripts; especially applied to those who wrote and copied prior to the invention of printing.

Stylus. A pre-modern writing implement with a pointed end for imprinting words on a wax tablet, and a spatula-shaped end for erasing the words.

Trivium. Upper division of the "seven liberal arts" which were considered essential for the development of the thinking skills that denoted a well-educated person in the classical and medieval period; the "Trivium" consisted of the study of three subjects: grammar, logic, and rhetoric.

Vellum. A writing surface usually made from prepared calf-skin, making it a material of higher quality than other parchments prepared from other animal skins.

Via affirmativa. An approach to the spiritual life, and the communication of it, that involves the employment of a multiplicity of images; based on the premise that God can be understood in all aspects of creation. Also known as *cataphatic* or *affective* spirituality.

Via negativa. An approach to the spiritual life, and the communication of it, that involves the stripping away of all material, mental, and emotional distractions, and all words and images and mediations that are so often used in drawing near to, and describing, the love of God. Also known as *apophatic* mysticism.

Viriditas. Originally from the Latin *viridi* meaning "greenness," and used by Gregory the Great (ca. 540–604 CE) to refer to spiritual health; the twelfth century abbess, Hildegard of Bingen, expanded the word's meaning in her writings to refer to the potential and possibility for growth and renewal in the spirit as well as in nature.

Vivified. Past tense of *vivify*, meaning to enliven, to come alive.